Rita Moreno

Consulting Editors

Hispanics of Achievement

Rita Moreno

Susan Suntree

Chelsea House Publishers
New York   Philadelphia

CHELSEA HOUSE PUBLISHERS

Editor-in-Chief: Richard S. Papale
Managing Editor: Karyn Gullen Browne
Copy Chief: Philip Koslow
Picture Editor: Adrian G. Allen
Assistant Art Director: Howard Brotman
Manufacturing Director: Gerald Levine
Systems Manager: Lindsey Ottman
Production Coordinator: Marie Claire Cebrián-Ume

Hispanics of Achievement
Senior Editor: John W. Selfridge

Staff for RITA MORENO
Copy Editor: David Carter
Designer: Rob Yaffe
Picture Researcher: Wendy P. Wills
Cover Illustration: Vilma Ortiz

First Printing

1 3 5 7 9 8 6 4 2

Library of Congress Cataloging-in-Publication Data
Suntree, Susan.
    Rita Moreno/Susan Suntree.
        p. cm.—(Hispanics of achievement)
    Includes bibliographical references and index.
    Summary: Examines the life and career of the Puerto Rican
singer and actress and discusses her accomplishments in theater,
television, and film.
    ISBN 0-7910-1247-6
         0-7910-1274-3(pbk.)
    1. Moreno, Rita—Juvenile literature. 2. Entertainers—Puerto
Rico—Biography—Juvenile literature. [1. Moreno, Rita. 2. Actors
and actresses. 3. Puerto Ricans—Biography.] I. Title. II. Series.
PN2334.M67S86 1992   91-37814
782.42164'092—dc20   CIP
    [B]   AC

96238

Contents

Hispanics of Achievement

Joan Baez
Mexican-American folksinger

Rubén Blades
Panamanian lawyer and entertainer

Jorge Luis Borges
Argentine writer

Juan Carlos
King of Spain

Pablo Casals
Spanish cellist and conductor

Miguel de Cervantes
Spanish writer

Cesar Chavez
Mexican-American labor leader

El Cid
Spanish military leader

Roberto Clemente
Puerto Rican baseball player

Salvador Dalí
Spanish painter

Plácido Domingo
Spanish singer

Gloria Estefan
Cuban-American singer

Gabriel García Márquez
Colombian writer

Pancho Gonzales
Mexican-American tennis player

Francisco José de Goya
Spanish painter

Frida Kahlo
Mexican painter

José Martí
Cuban revolutionary and poet

Rita Moreno
Puerto Rican singer and actress

Pablo Neruda
Chilean poet and diplomat

Antonia Novello
U.S. surgeon general

Octavio Paz
Mexican poet and critic

Pablo Picasso
Spanish artist

Anthony Quinn
Mexican-American actor

Oscar de la Renta
Dominican fashion designer

Diego Rivera
Mexican painter

Linda Ronstadt
Mexican-American singer

Antonio López de Santa Anna
Mexican general and politician

George Santayana
Spanish philosopher and poet

Andrés Segovia
Spanish guitarist

Junípero Serra
Spanish missionary and explorer

Lee Trevino
Mexican-American golfer

Diego Velázquez
Spanish painter

Pancho Villa
Mexican revolutionary

CHELSEA HOUSE PUBLISHERS

INTRODUCTION

Hispanics of Achievement

Rodolfo Cardona

The Spanish language and many other elements of Spanish culture are present in the United States today and have been since the
country's earliest beginnings. Some of these elements have come
directly from the Iberian Peninsula; others have come indirectly, by
way of Mexico, the Caribbean basin, and the countries of Central
and South America.

Spanish culture has influenced America in many subtle ways,
and consequently many Americans remain relatively unaware of
the extent of its impact. The vast majority of them recognize the
influence of Spanish culture in America, but they often do not
realize the great importance and long history of that influence.
This is partly because Americans have tended to judge the Hispanic
influence in the United States in statistical terms rather than
to look closely at the ways in which individual Hispanics have
profoundly affected American culture. For this reason, it is fitting

that Americans obtain more than a passing acquaintance with the origins of these Spanish cultural elements and gain an understanding of how they have been woven into the fabric of American society.

It is well documented that Spanish seafarers were the first to explore and colonize many of the early territories of what is today called the United States of America. For this reason, students of geography discover Hispanic names all over the map of the United States. For instance, the Strait of Juan de Fuca was named after the Spanish explorer who first navigated the waters of the Pacific Northwest; the names of states such as Arizona (arid zone), Montana (mountain), Florida (thus named because it was reached on Easter Sunday, which in Spanish is called the feast of Pascua Florida), and California (named after a fictitious land in one of the first and probably the most popular among the Spanish novels of chivalry, *Amadis of Gaul*) are all derived from Spanish; and there are numerous mountains, rivers, canyons, towns, and cities with Spanish names throughout the United States.

Not only explorers but many other illustrious figures in Spanish history have helped define American culture. For example, the 13th-century king of Spain, Alfonso X, also known as the Learned, may be unknown to the majority of Americans, but his work on the codification of Spanish law has greatly influenced the evolution of American law, particularly in the jurisdictions of the Southwest. For this contribution a statue of him stands in the rotunda of the Capitol in Washington, D.C. Likewise, the name Diego Rivera may be unfamiliar to most Americans, but this Mexican painter influenced many American artists whose paintings, commissioned during the Great Depression and the New Deal era of the 1930s, adorn the walls of government buildings throughout the United States. In recent years the contributions of Puerto Ricans, Mexicans, Mexican Americans (Chicanos), and Cubans in American cities such as Boston, Chicago, Los Angeles, Miami, Minneapolis, New York, and San Antonio have been enormous.

The importance of the Spanish language in this vast cultural complex cannot be overstated. Spanish, after all, is second only to English as the most widely spoken of Western languages within the United States as well as in the entire world. The popularity of the Spanish language in America has a long history.

In addition to Spanish exploration of the New World, the great Spanish literary tradition served as a vehicle for bringing the language and culture to America. Interest in Spanish literature in America began when English immigrants brought with them translations of Spanish masterpieces of the Golden Age. As early as 1683, private libraries in Philadelphia and Boston contained copies of the first picaresque novel, *Lazarillo de Tormes*, translations of Francisco de Quevedo's *Los Sueños*, and copies of the immortal epic of reality and illusion *Don Quixote*, by the great Spanish writer Miguel de Cervantes. It would not be surprising if Cotton Mather, the arch-Puritan, read *Don Quixote* in its original Spanish, if only to enrich his vocabulary in preparation for his writing *La fe del cristiano en 24 artículos de la Institución de Cristo, enviada a los españoles para que abran sus ojos* (The Christian's Faith in 24 Articles of the Institution of Christ, Sent to the Spaniards to Open Their Eyes), published in Boston in 1699.

Over the years, Spanish authors and their works have had a vast influence on American literature—from Washington Irving, John Steinbeck, and Ernest Hemingway in the novel to Henry Wadsworth Longfellow and Archibald MacLeish in poetry. Such important American writers as James Fenimore Cooper, Edgar Allan Poe, Walt Whitman, Mark Twain, and Herman Melville all owe a sizable debt to the Spanish literary tradition. Some writers, such as Willa Cather and Maxwell Anderson, who explored Spanish themes they came into contact with in the American Southwest and Mexico, were influenced less directly but no less profoundly.

Important contributions to a knowledge of Spanish culture in the United States were also made by many lesser known individuals—teachers, publishers, historians, entrepreneurs, and others—with a love for Spanish culture. One of the most significant of these contributions was made by Abiel Smith, a Harvard College graduate of the class of 1764, when he bequeathed stock worth $20,000 to Harvard for the support of a professor of French and Spanish. By 1819 this endowment had produced enough income to appoint a professor, and the philologist and humanist George Ticknor became the first holder of the Abiel Smith Chair, which was the very first endowed Chair at Harvard University. Other illustrious holders of the Smith Chair would include the poets Henry Wadsworth Longfellow and James Russell Lowell.

A highly respected teacher and scholar, Ticknor was also a collector of Spanish books, and as such he made a very special contribution to America's knowledge of Spanish culture. He was instrumental in amassing for Harvard libraries one of the first and most impressive collections of Spanish books in the United States. He also had a valuable personal collection of Spanish books and manuscripts, which he bequeathed to the Boston Public Library.

With the creation of the Abiel Smith Chair, Spanish language and literature courses became part of the curriculum at Harvard, which also went on to become the first American university to offer graduate studies in Romance languages. Other colleges and universities throughout the United States gradually followed Harvard's example, and today Spanish language and culture may be studied at most American institutions of higher learning.

No discussion of the Spanish influence in the United States, however brief, would be complete without a mention of the Spanish influence on art. Important American artists such as John Singer Sargent, James A. M. Whistler, Thomas Eakins, and Mary Cassatt all explored Spanish subjects and experimented with Spanish techniques. Virtually every serious American artist living today has studied the work of the Spanish masters as well as the great 20th-century Spanish painters Salvador Dalí, Joan Miró, and Pablo Picasso.

The most pervasive Spanish influence in America, however, has probably been in music. Compositions such as Leonard Bernstein's *West Side Story*, the Latinization of William Shakespeare's *Romeo and Juliet* set in New York's Puerto Rican quarter, and Aaron Copland's *Salon Mexico* are two obvious examples. In general, one can hear the influence of Latin rhythms—from tango to mambo, from guaracha to salsa—in virtually every form of American music.

This series of biographies, which Chelsea House has published under the general title HISPANICS OF ACHIEVEMENT, constitutes further recognition of—and a renewed effort to bring forth to the consciousness of America's young people—the contributions that Hispanic people have made not only in the United States but throughout the civilized world. The men and women who are featured in this series have attained a high level of accomplishment in their respective fields of endeavor and have made a permanent mark on American society.

The title of this series must be understood in its broadest possible sense: The term *Hispanics* is intended to include Spaniards, Spanish Americans, and individuals from many countries whose language and culture have either direct or indirect Spanish origins. The names of many of the people included in this series will be immediately familiar; others will be less recognizable. All, however, have attained recognition within their own countries, and often their fame has transcended their borders.

The series HISPANICS OF ACHIEVEMENT thus addresses the attainments and struggles of Hispanic people in the United States and seeks to tell the stories of individuals whose personal and professional lives in some way reflect the larger Hispanic experience. These stories are exemplary of what human beings can accomplish, often against daunting odds and by extraordinary personal sacrifice, where there is conviction and determination. Fray Junípero Serra, the 18th-century Spanish Franciscan missionary, is one such individual. Although in very poor health, he devoted the last 15 years of his life to the foundation of missions throughout California—then a mostly unsettled expanse of land—in an effort to bring a better life to Native Americans through the cultivation of crafts and animal husbandry. An example from recent times, the Mexican-American labor leader Cesar Chavez has battled bitter opposition and made untold personal sacrifices in his effort to help poor agricultural workers who have been exploited for decades on farms throughout the Southwest.

The talent with which each one of these men and women may have been endowed required dedication and hard work to develop and become fully realized. Many of them have enjoyed rewards for their efforts during their own lifetime, whereas others have died poor and unrecognized. For some it took a long time to achieve their goals, for others success came at an early age, and for still others the struggle continues. All of them, however, stand out as people whose lives have made a difference, whose achievements we need to recognize today and should continue to honor in the future.

Rita Moreno

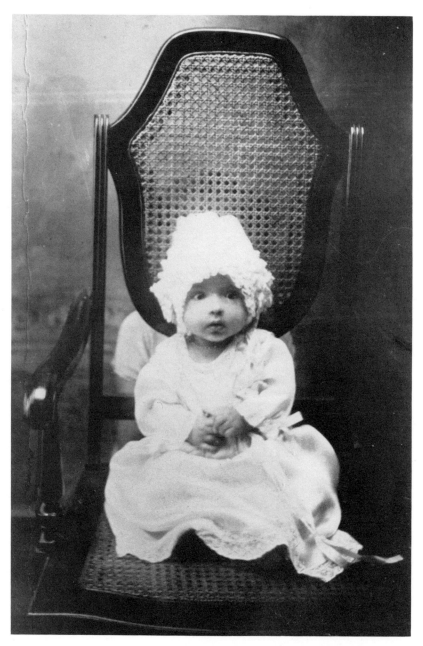

Rosa Dolores Alverio, later admired by millions as the talented singer, dancer, and actress Rita Moreno, was born on December 11, 1931, in Humacao, Puerto Rico. In 1936, Moreno and her mother, Rosa María, immigrated to New York in hopes of finding a better life.

CHAPTER ONE

Tropical Dreams

It was the winter of 1936, and the streets of New York City were glazed with slick, gray ice. The ambulance turned off Amsterdam Avenue and headed up 180th Street, a neighborhood lined with old, narrow tenements, four and five stories high. Most of the families living there were Puerto Ricans, the latest wave of poor immigrants looking for opportunity in the city where the Statue of Liberty lights the harbor.

The ambulance screeched to a stop, its doors swung open, and out jumped the driver and his partner, their clean white uniforms stark against the gray hues of the city. Neighbors, stirred by the noise and commotion in the street, pressed against frosty windows to watch the scene below. The two men entered one of the buildings, climbed the stairs, found the apartment they were looking for, and knocked loudly on the door.

A young Puerto Rican mother let them in and pointed to one of the bedrooms, where a five-year-old girl covered with red spots was sleeping on a bed in the corner. She had chicken pox. At that

An Upper West Side neighborhood in Manhattan. Rosa María and Rosita, as Moreno's mother called her, lived in a small room in this part of New York City during the 1930s and early 1940s. They sought opportunity, but their dreams quickly clashed with the harsh economic realities of the Great Depression.

time, the law required that anyone with a contagious disease such as chicken pox be quarantined; the girl would have to be taken away. But the girl's mother, worried and tearful, barely understood what the ambulance driver and his partner were telling her as she watched them carry her little Rosita Alverio out into the cold.

Waking to find herself wrapped in a blanket and in the arms of two strangers, Rosita kicked and struggled to unwrap herself. But the men easily kept her from doing so and placed her in the back of the ambulance. She tried to make sense of what the men were saying but could not, and she was barely able to see them, her head half covered by the blanket. Then, through her fever and fear, she heard the sudden wail of a siren and felt a jolt as the ambulance carried her away.

In the children's ward, Rosita watched everything from her hospital bed. The room was warm and well lighted, but she remained confused and afraid, not knowing exactly why she had to be taken from her mother and wondering what was to become of her. She tried to talk to a boy in the next bed, but she spoke no English and he no Spanish. Every time she tried to talk to him, he would say, "Shut up! Shut up!" These were the first English words she learned. Alone and unable to communicate with those around her, Rosita curled up in her hospital bed and dreamed about her home, the beautiful Caribbean island of Puerto Rico.

Rosita, whose full name was Rosa Dolores Alverio, was born on December 11, 1931, in Humacao, a little village nestled next to a rain forest. Nearby, a mountain called El Yunque rose out of the thick jungle into the tropical sunlight.

Trinidad López, Rosita's maternal grandmother, was a fair-skinned woman of Spanish descent. Rosita's mother, Rosa María Marcano, married Paco Alverio when she was still a teenager. Alverio's family were *jíbaros*, the name used to refer to the people who lived outside Puerto Rico's major towns and cities. Jíbaros valued their independence and strove to be self-sufficient, preferring to grow crops on their own small farms rather than work on the large coffee or sugar plantations of the wealthy.

Christopher Columbus, a Genoese who sailed under the Spanish flag during the late 15th century, and his crew were the first Europeans to see Puerto Rico. On his second voyage through the Caribbean Islands, in 1493, Columbus was awed by their lush beauty and moved by the dignity and grace of the native Indians. Though Columbus himself never set foot on the shores of Puerto Rico, or Borinquén as the natives called it, his men did, and they returned to the ship with tales of a strange and fascinating island culture. They told of how the native Indians, or Tainos, worshiped a mother goddess who was believed to live with her male partner, the fire god Yo Cahu, on El Yunque, the mountain that towered over the village where Rosita and her family lived. Unlike in Spain, women played a prominent role in Borinquén political life, enjoying many freedoms and holding positions of great power and influence.

Spain invaded and conquered Puerto Rico in 1509, and those who resisted were forced into hiding in the mountains. Before long, Spanish colonists and the Tainos began to intermarry. The Spanish brought Africans to the island as slaves to work the gold mines and sugar plantations. Slaves who managed to escape joined those who had fled to the mountains, where African, Indian, and European blood combined to create the jibaros, the first Puerto Ricans.

In 1898, the U.S. government, influenced by investors and businessmen in the United States who wanted to control Puerto Rican and Cuban sugar plantations and natural resources, launched a propaganda campaign that swayed the American people against Spain. The United States declared war on Spain and invaded Puerto Rico as part of its effort to annex Cuba. After the invasion, a military council was set up to rule the island, and Puerto Rico has remained an American colony ever since. The jibaros watched as one conqueror replaced another.

All the conflicts of Puerto Rico's history were reflected in the Alverio household. Rosita lived with her parents and her younger brother, Francisco, in a tiny white stucco house in Humacao. The family was very poor, but because everyone in the village lived simply, Rosita never thought of herself as deprived.

Rosita loved the warm, fragrant jungle that surrounded her village. When she was only three years old, her mother asked her to entertain the neighbors, whom she easily impressed with her ability to name many of the plants in the forest near their house. Her mother would snap off a small branch and give it to Rosita. The little girl would hold it in her hand, sometimes smell it, and then, to everyone's delight, accurately name the plant.

The family cooked on a charcoal fire built on a special table in the kitchen of their house. Rosita and her brother slept in bunk beds. Because they did not have indoor plumbing, the family used an outhouse. Wash day was always fun for Rosita because she enjoyed helping her mother carry the family's dirty laundry to a nearby stream and then wading and splashing as her mother soaped and rubbed the clothes on the wet rocks. When the washing was done, Rosita helped her mother hang the clothes out to dry on tree branches.

Ironing, on the other hand, was not so enjoyable. Because there were no electric irons, Rosita's mother used heavy, old-fashioned metal ones. She would place her irons in sand that was heated by the sun. As the sun beat down on the sand, the irons became hot, and she would use one iron at a time to press the clothes.

Rosita always enjoyed family gatherings, which often included the neighbors as well. The children would play games as everyone sang, ate, and danced. Occasionally, someone would put on a record, and everyone clapped when little Rosita danced around for her grandparents. No one in her family was particularly musical, but everyone loved singing and dancing.

Surrounded by the lush greenery of rural Puerto Rico, men work the fields as family members look on. Growing up in urban America, the young Rita Moreno often pined for her idyllic homeland, with its beautiful landscape and pleasant climate.

Rosita's early childhood was fun and carefree, but harder times for the Alverio family were in the offing. Things began to turn sour when Rosita's parents divorced. Rosita was only four years old.

By the mid-1930s, Puerto Ricans were finding it more difficult than ever to make a living. The jibaros, especially, felt the terrible effects of economic hardship, made worse by the U.S. government's practice of flooding Puerto Rican farmlands for dams, power plants, and other large-scale projects. Many jibaros left their homes in the country to seek job opportunities in town. Faced with the prospect of having no work at all, many Puerto Ricans left the island for the ghettos of New York City, hoping to find work there.

Rosa María Alverio's problem was more complicated than that of the average Puerto Rican woman of the time: she was a single mother. Moreover, she was a single mother in a society that had not grown to accept the idea of women working outside the home. Over the years, Puerto Ricans had adopted the Spanish attitude that authority in the family and most of the power in the community belonged to men. Puerto Rican women were expected to raise children, cook, and clean. If a woman needed to earn a wage to support her family and could find a job, she did unskilled work at the lowest wages.

Rosa María, along with many other Puerto Ricans, decided to go to New York City, where she expected to find greater opportunity and few barriers to working women. When she boarded the boat for New York, she was very poor and only 19 years old. Perhaps Rosa María's courage to struggle for a better life had its roots in what a Spanish explorer described as the Borinquén Indians' ability to fight with a "strange fury." Upon her arrival, she moved in with her aunt, Tomasita López, and found a job sewing in a lingerie factory. She worked there for a year, saving all the money she could.

Meanwhile, in Puerto Rico, Rosita and Francisco lived with their father and his girlfriend. Then, about a year later, the children were surprised by their mother's return to Puerto Rico. She arrived

The Statue of Liberty. A symbol of freedom and opportunity for all, the statue greeted Rosita, her mother, and millions of other immigrants to the United States as they entered New York Harbor.

with a suitcase filled with presents and toys, and she had saved enough money to bring one of her children back to New York with her. Her plan was to return again a year later to fetch her remaining child.

All the gifts and the stories about America delighted the children. Rosita found her mother an exciting, exotic woman and was eager to go to America with her; Francisco, however, was less enthusiastic about leaving Puerto Rico. He had grown very close to his father and did not want to leave his home. Soon little Rosita and her mother boarded a huge ship filled with Puerto Ricans and bound for America.

Most of the people aboard ship were jibaros who had lost their jobs and their land. All hoped for a better life in America. As the ship slowly pulled out of San Juan Harbor, Rosita watched Puerto Rico slip into the past: she never saw her father or brother again.

A precocious Rosita (right) in a gypsy costume with a friend on a New York City rooftop. Life was very difficult for newly arrived immigrants to the United States during the 1930s; most could not find work and, like Rosita and her mother, were forced to live in crowded tenements.

CHAPTER TWO

Mean Streets

The voyage to New York was a nightmare for Rosa María and little Rosita. For 12 days the ship rolled and heaved through hurricane-driven storms. When they finally reached New York Harbor and were greeted by the Statue of Liberty, Rosita and her mother were grateful to be alive. But rough seas still lay ahead for the young Puerto Rican mother and her little girl.

Rosa María and Rosita arrived at Aunt Tomasita's apartment in Manhattan's Washington Heights section, and the two of them settled into one small room. Living conditions were crowded and uncomfortable, and there was now no lush world of green to which she could escape. Worse, Rosita had to be hospitalized for chicken pox soon after she and her mother arrived. But not long after Rosita came home from the hospital her mother married Enrique Cossio, a Cuban watchmaker. They moved into Enrique's apartment, and life improved.

As Puerto Rican immigrants arrived in New York City in increasing numbers, many moved into Washington Heights and the surrounding Upper West Side of Manhattan. The most popular part of the city for Puerto Rican immigrants was roughly the area between Fifth and Eighth avenues from 110th to 116th streets. This section of town eventually came to be known as *el barrio* (the neighborhood), a community where the native language was Spanish and the way of life was distinctly Puerto Rican. Rosita lived in a neighboring community, Washington Heights, that was very much like el barrio.

By the late 1930s, the United States was suffering from a severe economic depression, and many of the country's newly arrived immigrants could not find work. Those who were able to find jobs were usually employed in menial, low-paying occupations that had once been filled by the Irish, Italian, and Jewish immigrants who came before them. The Puerto Ricans mostly worked as janitors, as hotel maids, on the waterfront, or in the garment industry.

When Rosita's mother first came to Nueva York, as the Puerto Ricans called the city, she did piecework for 10 hours a day, sewing

Women toil over their sewing machines at a union shop in New York City. When she first came to New York, Rosa María did piecework at a garment factory for 10 hours a day, and because her shop was not unionized, management pursued profits at the expense of the security and safety of workers.

lingerie in a garment factory. (Doing piecework means that one is paid by the number of pieces completed each day or each week.) Consequently, none of the workers in Rosa María's shop took breaks, not even to eat. Moreover, because there was no union organized at the shop, management pursued profit and ignored such concerns as worker health and safety. There was no sense of job security among the workers, and the lack of disability and health insurance put workers' children at great risk. In short, the workers labored hard for many hours each day without a break, with no security, for very little money.

Living conditions for the laboring immigrant population were no better than the poor working conditions they endured. After work, people went home to cramped, dilapidated tenements. Often there was no heat or hot water, and usually several families shared a single apartment.

Teenagers from immigrant families had great difficulty finding jobs and consequently spent much of their time on the streets. Many formed or joined street gangs, which gave them a sense of identity and a feeling of belonging. The world of street gangs was a violent one in which fights in back alleys and schoolyards—often with bottles, clubs, chains, and even knives—were commonplace. Puerto Ricans also clashed with gangs outside their neighborhoods because many communities shunned and taunted the new immigrants. Even young children like Rosita were taunted with names like "pierced ears" and "gold teeth."

As the weather grew warmer, el barrio residents emerged from inside their apartments to the tenement stoops and at least by day took their neighborhoods back from the gangs. Boys played baseball, a game invented in the United States but popular in Puerto Rico since the 19th century. On the streets of New York, however, baseball usually meant stickball, where a batter steps up to a sewer cover and swings an old broom handle at a pink, or sometimes black, rubber ball. Rosita and her new friends played hopscotch or jump rope, or just sat on the crowded stoop and

Rosita and her mother on Jones Beach, Long Island, during the 1930s. When Rosa María married Enrique Cossio, a Cuban watchmaker, she and Rosita moved to his apartment in New York's Washington Heights section.

watched the people and cars go by. With television not yet invented, people turned to one another for entertainment. When they gathered on the stoops, few people ever complained about the hardships, preferring to forget about their troubles and enjoy themselves.

One day, Rosita's mother took her for a walk to a roof garden playground where children were playing. Rosa María sat with Rosita for a while and then said that she was going to buy some gum and would be right back. After she left, Rosita continued watching the other children from the steps. Eventually, a teacher called to the children and they gathered to go inside. Then the teacher walked over and spoke to Rosita in English, saying that it was time to go in now. Not understanding, she just sat still and looked up at the teacher. When the teacher urged her again, Rosita protested in Spanish, "No! No! I have to wait here for my mama. She's gone to get me some Chiclets." But the teacher managed to make a tearful Rosita go into the classroom. Rosita was certain that she would never see her mother again.

When Rosita's mother returned to pick her up at the end of that first frightening school day, Rosita was angry and hurt. It had all been a trick: expecting her daughter to put up resistance at the idea of going to school, Rosa María had fooled Rosita to get her there. Though Rosa María had not intended to upset Rosita, by tricking her daughter into going to school she had made the experience more stressful for Rosita than it already was.

In the late 1930s, New York schools, including Public School 132, which Rosita attended, did not have bilingual education. Nobody helped Rosita learn English; she had to pick it up as quickly as she could, however she could. Understandably, Rosita was quiet in the classroom, never volunteering answers and rarely speaking at all unless she had to. Slowly, her English improved: she proved herself a good speller, and eventually she became fluent in English, mainly by practicing at home.

Arithmetic was another story. Rosita thought numbers behaved by magic and that people got the right answers to mathematics problems by tuning in to that magic. When the teacher gave her figures and asked for their sum, Rosita called out any number that came into her head. All her answers were wrong, and it never occurred to the teacher that Rosita did not understand English well enough to grasp her explanations.

Because no teacher or counselor took an individual interest in her or recognized her special needs and talents, Rosita remained very self-conscious throughout her school years. The trauma of trying to learn English and her lessons at the same time was very painful, and she began to doubt her own abilities. She rarely put up her hand to answer a question because she was afraid of answering incorrectly.

Outside the classroom, however, Rosita was not as shy. Whenever there was a talent show or school assembly, she would gladly perform the Mexican hat dance or sing a song. Although she matured naturally along with the other girls, Rosita did not grow as quickly as her schoolmates, and she worried that she would always

Rosita (center) poses with her classmates, some of whom are in costume for a school play. Having arrived in the United States speaking virtually no English, Rosita was a quiet pupil who rarely volunteered answers in class. When dancing on stage, however, she was far less shy.

be small. She did not let this stop her, however, from becoming an energetic and vibrant performer. The praise and success Rosita longed for but did not find in her studies came at an early age from her work as a performer.

Rosita's mother had a friend, Irene López, who was a Spanish dancer. When Irene watched little six-year-old Rosita dance to records in the living room, she would say to Rosa María, "You ought to take Rosita to dancing class. She's a natural!" After some thought, Rosa María decided to send her daughter for dance lessons. Maybe, she thought, Rosita could escape the tenements by becoming a famous Spanish dancer.

The decision to send Rosita for lessons was a difficult one because Rosa María was earning only a small amount making crepe-paper flowers at home for the Woolworth Company. But Enrique was working steadily as a watchmaker, and in the end the family was able to scrape enough money together to send Rosita to Paco Cansino, the actress Rita Hayworth's uncle, for Spanish dancing lessons.

Cansino taught Rosita intensively, having her learn at least one dance every three classes. Consequently, little Rosita's repertoire grew quickly even though she went to class only once a week. When he decided she was ready, Cansino took Rosita to a nightclub in the Greenwich Village section of New York, where they danced the *sevillanas* together and played castanets. The audience loved watching an accomplished professional dancing with his sparkling seven-year-old partner. This was Rosita's first public performance.

Cansino recognized Rosita's talent and dedication, and he continued to teach her for several years. It became clear, however, that Rosita needed to learn other types of dance besides Spanish dancing, so she began to take tap lessons as well. Since she was already studying flamenco, which requires a lot of heel work, Rosita learned tap easily. Then she enrolled in ballet classes at a small conservatory. In addition to ballet, she studied what was called recitation. Rosita would stand up alone and sing a song or repeat lines she had memorized. Training in acting or singing was not included, but she had lots of practice performing because the conservatory had a children's theater in the toy department in Macy's.

When Rosita was eight, her mother began taking her to radio auditions after school. Sometimes they would make the rounds of the talent agencies, dropping off a picture and a résumé at each stop. An agency would call to set up an audition when a part that

Rosita (right) and a friend, two aspiring dancers, pose on a New York City rooftop. Rosita began dance lessons when she was five years old, studying Spanish dancing with Paco Cansino, who eventually included her in his act at a Greenwich Village nightclub, her first public performance.

seemed right was available. Performers usually did not sign with an agency as they do now. Every day Rosita's mother would read *Cue*, a show business magazine, where auditions were announced. Then she would take Rosita to the ones that looked promising, mostly those for radio shows. The radio program auditions were what is known in show business as "cattle calls." This meant that nobody had an appointment, that people just showed up, sometimes by the hundreds, and waited their turn to read from a script for a minute or two in front of the producers.

Rosita was cast in a variety of programs for both Spanish- and English-speaking audiences, singing Spanish songs and playing the castanets. From the time she was 11 until she was 15, Rosita dubbed voices in American films to be exported to Spanish-speaking countries. She was the Spanish-speaking voice of such well-known performers as Elizabeth Taylor, Margaret O'Brien, Peggy Ann Garner, and Judy Garland. Occasionally she was hired to sing and dance at weddings and bar mitzvahs, sometimes wearing a fancy banana headdress like the famous Latina dancing star Carmen Miranda. Once she was hired by the "Ave Maria Radio Hour," a Catholic program, to play Bernadette, a little French girl who had a vision. Because the producers had no idea what kind of accent Bernadette had, Rosita made up one, and everyone loved it.

Although she never forced Rosita to audition, Rosa María was anxious for her to succeed, believing that her daughter's talent could be their means of escaping poverty. She told Rosita repeatedly that if she wanted success, she would have to work hard for it, and she made her work very hard.

From the time she was eight years old, Rosita was very busy with her schoolwork, dance lessons, and auditions. In rare moments of leisure, she sometimes yearned to be back in Puerto Rico, with its mountains, forests, and pleasant climate. She remembered how as a little girl the pungent smell of jungle plants filled her nose, and thoughts of her father and brother would come upon her suddenly as she recalled the carefree days of her early childhood.

Rosita and her mother at a resort in the Pocono Mountains of Pennsylvania. When Rosita was eight years old, her mother began taking her to radio auditions and talent agencies, hoping to get her into show business. Rosa María pushed her daughter to work very hard.

These moments were few and far between, however, and her career put demands on her time that were increasingly difficult to meet. Rosita realized later that her effort to keep a busy schedule as a young girl was partly an attempt to prove to herself and others that she was indeed a person of exceptional talent. Throughout her childhood, she was haunted by feelings of inadequacy and worked hard to win the approval of others, particularly of her mother, who was very critical of her daughter, demanding near perfection from her in everything she did.

Of course, no one is perfect, but Rosita worked hard each day to get as close as possible to the high standards her mother demanded of her. As a result, Rosita came to resent her mother. On the inside, she struggled with conflicting emotions; on the outside, she never stopped smiling.

So, it was bound to happen. Rosita was doing well getting parts on radio variety shows and in commercials in both Spanish and English. When Rosita's mother read the announcement of an audition for a Broadway play, she closed *Cue* magazine and without hesitating said, "We're going."

Although she was entirely unschooled in acting, Rosita made her Broadway debut at the age of 13 as Angelina in the play Skydrift. *A beaming Rosa María watched her daughter from the audience on opening night; it was the first play she had ever attended.*

CHAPTER THREE

Broadway and Back

Rosita was 13 years old when, for the first time, she and her mother walked into the offices of a Broadway production company. The producers were looking for an 11-year-old "Italian-looking" girl for an upcoming war drama, *Skydrift*, that was to feature the actor Eli Wallach in his first Broadway show. Rosita looked young for her age and had dark hair, so they auditioned her. She and her mother were thrilled when they heard that Rosita got the part.

Rosita had always expected that if she were to get a big break, she would get it through her dancing. It was accepted at the time that as Puerto Rican boys could pull themselves out of poverty by excelling in boxing or baseball, girls could achieve success by becoming exceptional dancers. Although Rosita was entirely un-schooled in acting, she was about to make her Broadway debut. Her daughter's sudden plunge into acting surprised Rosa María; *Skydrift* was the first play Rosita's mother ever attended.

Skydrift was a World War II drama about young soldiers who had died in battle returning home one last time to say good-bye.

Rosita played the youngest sister of an Italian soldier. She adapted quickly to the rehearsals. Even though she had never performed in such a huge theater in front of so many people, Rosita showed no sign of stage fright. Granted, her part was a small one; she only had to say a few lines and eat spaghetti.

Rosita's naïveté got her into trouble during a preview, a performance before the play's official opening night. The audience was growing restless, stirring in their seats, and coughing while Lilly Valente, the lead actress, was saying her lines with great emotion. Rosita decided that she had to do something to save the scene. She started eating her spaghetti by sucking in the long strands or dropping it into her mouth from her fork, which she held above her head. Later, backstage, Valente grabbed Rosita and furiously intoned, "If you ever, ever do that again, anywhere in the world, I will hear about it, and you will die. I'll see to it."

Rosita was terrified and horribly embarrassed. She wanted to explain that she thought she was helping. If the audience would not be moved to tears, Rosita had thought, then maybe they would laugh. But she said nothing, and she never again attempted to interfere with a scene, no matter what. Despite her shame, Rosita did not run off the set or think about quitting but stayed and saw the show through to the end.

For *Skydrift*, the end was not so far away. It closed in November 1945, after only seven performances. Although the play was not successful, for Rosita it was the beginning of a long acting career that brought her back to Broadway many times.

Around this time, not only did Rosita's professional life change dramatically, but her family life changed as well. When Rosita was 12 years old, she and her mother went to an audition at a radio station, where they met a Mexican radio personality named Edward Moreno. Moreno was an intelligent, self-involved man with an interest in philosophy and the occult. Before long, Rosa María fell deeply in love with Moreno and left Enrique.

A pert Rosita poses on the stoop of her family's Valley Stream, Long Island, home during the late 1940s. In 1944, Rosa María decided to leave her husband and move to Valley Stream with her lover Edward Moreno, a radio personality, who eventually became Rosita's second stepfather.

Rosita was angry with her mother for leaving Enrique, whom she loved dearly and who had been the only father she had really known. She also blamed Moreno for the breakup of her family. Consequently, when they moved into a little house in Valley Stream, Long Island, they had their share of domestic tension. Rosa María's decision to move in with Moreno further angered and confused Rosita because by doing so her mother had broken a rule that up until then she had always lived by: Never move in with a man without marrying him first. Eventually Rosa María and Edward did marry, and they had a son, Dennis Moreno.

Rosita was busier than ever after the move to Long Island. She would occasionally help her mother with the baby, but most of the time she was occupied with schoolwork and auditions. When she was 13 years old, a talent scout from Metro-Goldwyn-Mayer (MGM) Studios came to her dancing school recital. Before he left, he gave his card to Rosita's mother. During the next few years, he would call occasionally to see if Rosita was still performing.

Just before the family left Washington Heights, Rosita had enrolled in a private school for children in the performing arts, the Professional Children's School. On a typical school day, she was up by six to catch the train into Manhattan. Classes started at eight, and by one o'clock the schoolday was finished. Sometimes her mother would take the train into town to meet Rosita after school and accompany her on visits to agencies, dancing lessons, and auditions, or calls, as they are known in the industry.

Rosita felt out of place at the Professional Children's School. To her, the other students, who were mostly actors, seemed very sophisticated and confident. Rosita felt more like a little street dancer than a professional actor. She felt left out and lonely. After a few years, Rosita transferred to another professional school, the Burton School.

Rosita was not happy as a teenager. She enjoyed working toward a career in show business, but the joys of performing could only be gained after one experienced many rejections. Competition was stiff at every audition; sometimes hundreds would compete for only one or two spots. The constant hustle for work in such a competitive profession frequently dampened Rosita's spirits, so each weekend she went to the movies to take her mind off the demands of her career.

From the time she was nine years old, Rosita spent every Saturday at the movies with her mother or her friends. A ticket to see the show—which always included a double feature, trailers, a comedy short, and a newsreel—only cost a quarter. A hot dog and a soda each cost a nickel. Rosita loved everything about the movies, which stirred her imagination and opened up new worlds to her. Like many young girls, she sat wide-eyed and swooning as the handsome leading man carried the beautiful leading lady off into the sunset. Rosita dreamed of being swept off her feet just as the young women on the silver screen were. She also dreamed about fame, jewels, and fancy clothes. One of her very favorite films was *Imitation of Life*, which was later remade starring the glamorous Lana Turner, Rosita's film idol.

Like so many immigrants to the United States, and especially people of color, Rosita struggled to assimilate—to suppress her true self, to deny her Puerto Rican heritage, and to conform to the mainstream American ideal. She set her hair around orange juice cans to straighten it, and she wore pink poodle skirts with white blouses. In *Imitation of Life* the protagonist is a woman who hides the fact that she has black African blood and eventually rejects her mother. Rosita was deeply moved by this story and never forgot it. Not only did the mother-daughter conflict in the film touch her, but so did its theme that one could be so ashamed of one's bloodline that one would do almost anything to hide it.

As a teenager, Rosita was so involved in her career that she never had a boyfriend or even went to a dance. But she was intrigued by the children who lived in Valley Stream because they seemed so unlike those she knew on Amsterdam Avenue. Her new neighbors were mostly working-class and middle-income families

The actress Lana Turner sits for a lighting test on the Hollywood set of Imitation of Life. *In 1948, 17-year-old Rosita, who idolized glamorous actesses such as Turner and Elizabeth Taylor, met MGM Studios magnate Louis B. Mayer, who offered her a contract.*

of Italian, Jewish, and Irish backgrounds. Rosita felt so unsure of herself that she hardly knew how to handle even the little social life she had. Once, when she was about 15 years old, she had the chance to go to a prom. Later, she recalled, "Two of the boys from the neighborhood came to my house and asked my mother if they could see me. I went into a huge panic, so she told them to just hang on a moment, and closed the door and told me, 'There are two boys here.' I felt so ugly. I went into such a panic because I didn't have any makeup on. I ran into the bathroom and slapped pancake makeup on my face. I made them wait at least 15 minutes. When I finally went out to see them, they invited me to a dance at their high school, and I said OK. But when that evening arrived, I got so scared that when they came to the door, I told my mother to tell them I couldn't go."

Rosita did not have her first real date with a young man until she was 17 years old and a talent agent in his early twenties asked her out. To Rosita, he seemed American—tall, handsome, blond, square jawed, and terribly attractive. They arranged to meet at Madison Square Garden to see a circus. When he was late, Rosita was ready to burst into tears; pacing and wringing her hands, she was certain that he was not going to show up. For years afterward, she felt a terrible sense of abandonment whenever her date was even a few minutes late. About 15 minutes later, the young man arrived, but Rosita had a difficult time relaxing after she had worked herself into such an emotional state. She later recalled, "We went out three or four more times but he couldn't get anywhere with me. I was virginal and truly very innocent. When he gave me a real kiss for the first time, I thought I would die of disgust. He opened his mouth! All he met was clenched teeth."

Rosita was attracted to him but afraid of what she might be getting into, unable to get over the sexual confusion most adolescents know all too well. For years her mother had cautioned her about men, saying that they could be very attractive but also dangerous in that they could get a girl into a lot of trouble, but she was never more specific. Once her mother gave her a book about farm animals as an attempt to explain sex, but it was not of much use to her. "I needed a boy my age who was as [innocent] as I was at my age. But as it turned out, I never went out with a boy my age, ever."

When she was 16 years old, Rosita wanted a drastic change in her life. She quit high school and decided to quit show business too. Rosa María did not protest her daughter's decision to quit school. Her response was simply, "Well, you're going to have to work if you're going to do that." She then asked Rosita what kind of work she was going to do. Rosita answered that she would be a secretary, and she promptly enrolled in a typing class. After a week, she realized secretarial work was not for her. She quit the class and was back to her rounds of auditions and agencies. As it turned out, unlike most actors and dancers, who seem to change their line of work almost as often as they change makeup, she never held any other job but performing.

One of Rosita's agents, George Libby, thought she could do well for herself by performing in nightclubs. Even though she was only 16, he lined up a series of spots for her in variety acts in Massachusetts, Pennsylvania, New Jersey, and Canada, where she was not underage. In a typical evening, a nightclub show would include a band, a Spanish dancer, a comic, and an accordion player. Rosita, of course, would be the Spanish dancer.

Although she already had a job singing in a Latin band in the Bronx when Libby made the suggestion, she decided to give nightclubs a try. She put together some dances she had learned from Paco Cansino, from whom she continued to take lessons, and paid a piano player to write an arrangement for her. When she arrived at the nightclub, she would hand her music to the musicians and when it was her turn, she would dance flamenco to the oddly suited accompaniment of a piano, an accordion, and a bass, the typical nightclub band. Once, when she did perform in New York, where she was underage, the police raided the club. The owner quickly wrapped her in a mink coat and sat her in a dark corner with a drink until the police left.

As she got used to the nightclub routine, Rosita played up her "Latin spitfire" reputation because it got her work and attention. At that time, fiery Latin actresses like Carmen Miranda and Lupe Velez were extremely popular. One of the New Jersey clubs Rosita played was decorated like a jungle. When the owners, reputedly mobsters, wanted to bill her as "Rosita the Cheetah," she did not object.

Dancing in nightclubs was hard work. Rosita spent hours alone on buses and trains. She was only five feet two inches tall and slight of build, yet everywhere she went she had to carry two enormous

After appearing in her first film, a New York reform school drama entitled So Young So Bad, *in 1949, Rosita prepared to move to California to make her debut as a Hollywood movie actress. To Rosita, life seemed full of promise.*

suitcases, filled with her heavy costumes and street clothes. Often she would arrive in Valley Stream at 3:00 A.M., exhausted from carrying her bags on and off buses and subways. Her parents never offered to meet her or help her. She was on her own.

When Rosita was 17 years old, the MGM talent scout who had been calling her mother faithfully since Rosita was 13 called again with big news. Louis B. Mayer, the head of MGM Studios, was in New York, and the scout had arranged for Rosita to meet him. Rosita went to the meeting accompanied by her mother and her current nightclub agent, Lenny Green, who was stunned to be able to meet the famous film mogul. Rosita, no Latin spitfire this time, was perfectly sweet and charming at the meeting. She wanted to look like Elizabeth Taylor, so she carefully dressed and made herself up to look like the famous star, going so far as to wear a waist cincher to copy Taylor's figure. To her satisfaction, at the meeting Mayer observed that she looked like a Latin Liz Taylor. Mayer, who impressed a naive Rosita as being a nice, fatherly Jewish man, liked her, liked her agent, and signed her to a standard seven-year young performer's contract. Rosita was thrilled beyond words. On December 26, 1949, shortly after her 18th birthday, a brief article in the *New York Times* announced that Rosita Moreno had received a Christmas present from MGM Studios, a contract that started at $200 a week and was expected to graduate to $1,500.

But Rosita could not leave for Hollywood yet because she had to stay in New York to finish making her first film. She had been cast as one of the delinquents in the black-and-white reform school drama, *So Young So Bad.* As she prepared to move to Los Angeles, Rosita wrote a letter to a girlfriend. "It was a really wonderful teenage letter. It was handwritten on lined paper and must have been 12 pages long talking about how my life was about to begin, and how I was going to do this, and I was going to do that. Great things were going to happen. I was just filled with the glory, and the thrill, and the fantasy of all this."

Moreno in a 1953 promotional photograph for Columbia Pictures. Although she accepted roles that stereotyped Latin women as dark, passionate temptresses, Moreno constantly struggled to break down such clichés and play richer and more diverse characters.

CHAPTER FOUR

Rita the Cheetah

In 1950, Rosita moved to Los Angeles, taking her Spanish dancing dresses, shoes, and spitfire reputation with her. Her stepfather, who had been working as a writer as well as a radio host, supported the move because he thought it might be good for his career as well.

Rosita, her mother, and her half brother Dennis settled into a little cottage in Culver City, California, near the MGM studios. Edward joined them a few months later after selling the house in Valley Stream. About a year after Edward arrived in Los Angeles, he decided to join the army so he could go to Japan, where he felt he could advance his career. Rosa María did not want to go to Japan. She wanted to stay in Los Angeles with Rosita. Edward left, and soon they divorced.

On their own again, Rosita and her mother lived very frugally. Rosa María went back to work for the first time in several years, first as a seamstress, later as a cook, and eventually at several other jobs. As a contract player, Rosita earned a salary from MGM. Five days a week she went to the studio to study dancing and acting.

For a few years, Rosita had been using her stepfather's surname, which the studio liked. But shortly after she arrived it was suggested that she shorten her first name to Rita. From then on, she was billed as Rita Moreno.

For Moreno, the studio seemed bursting with possibility. On her first day, she was given a tour and introduced to several movie stars and other important people in the movie industry. Soon she was cast in a small part in a Mario Lanza film.

Lanza was a very popular opera tenor-turned-actor who had been signed by MGM. In *The Toast of New Orleans*, Lanza's second film, made in 1950, Moreno played a young Cajun, Tina, who is madly in love with Lanza's character but loses him to another woman, played by Kathryn Grayson. Moreno was terrified when the choreographer teamed her with James Mitchell, a well-trained ballet dancer from New York. When the choreographer asked her to demonstrate her dance training, Moreno gulped, asked for some Latin music, and improvised some show-style Latin shakes and shimmies. Moreno knew the studio thought she had training in dancing and acting that she did not have. Nevertheless, her dance

Rosita and her mother in Los Angeles in 1950. That year, Rosita changed her name to Rita Moreno and made her Hollywood film debut as Tina in The Toast of New Orleans, *with the dashing opera-singer-turned-actor Mario Lanza.*

Moreno demonstrates the rumba with actor Keith Larsen in the early 1950s. Moreno's dancing skills were put to good use in The Toast of New Orleans *when the film's choreographer teamed her with James Mitchell, a New York ballet dancer, in a dance sequence.*

sequence with James Mitchell was a success. That year, Esther Williams, the swimmer-turned-movie star, made a musical aquatic extravaganza, *Pagan Love Song*, and Rita played a native girl.

After *Pagan Love Song* was completed, Moreno began to sense that something was wrong. Because her contract had nearly run its course, she went to see the head of casting, Billy Grady, to ask what was next for her. Getting no definite answer, she approached him numerous times. A month went by, and Grady finally told her, "Honey, who're you kiddin'? They're gonna drop you like a bad habit."

Moreno was devastated. After less than two years with MGM, her chance for a successful movie career seemed to be over. Not only did she lose her income, but what only a short time ago seemed a very promising future now looked bleak. It was difficult for her to face her mother.

Moreno was determined to rebuild her career. After all, she was only 19 years old, she had gained valuable experience at MGM,

Moreno strikes an alluring pose on the set of Pagan Love Song, *which was filmed in Hawaii and was her first picture shot on location. That year she received the disappointing news that her MGM contract would not be renewed.*

and, most important, she was enormously talented. She contacted her agent, who immediately set about finding work for her. The parts he found, however, were what Moreno called "jobs"—parts in television serials and B movies—not roles that would build a career. She took them because she needed money and because she desperately wanted to stay in the movie business.

Now 20 years old, Moreno decided to move out of her mother's place and share an apartment with a friend. On her own for the first time, Moreno went to work doing television shows, collecting unemployment checks when work was slow, and auditioning for films. She managed to get the role of Zelda Zanders in a production of the classic MGM musical *Singin' in the Rain.* Usually, however, she was cast as the stereotypical spicy Latin or native temptress in B movies with titles like *The Fabulous Señorita* (Republic, 1952), *The Ring* (King Brothers, 1952), and *Cattle Town* (Warner, 1952).

Breaking the mold seemed impossible. Moreno continued to be cast as a quick-tempered Latina with flaring nostrils wearing what she later called the Rita Moreno costume—an off-the-shoulder peasant blouse, dangling earrings, and sandals or, often, no shoes at all. In 1953, she was cast in MGM's film *Latin Lovers*. She also played Maroa in Paramount's *Jivaro* (1954), set in a Latin American jungle. According to the Hollywood movie establishment, any dark-eyed, dark-haired non-Anglo was interchangeable with any other, so Moreno was cast as an Arab for Columbia's war drama *El Alamein* (1953). She played a Native American in *Fort Vengeance* (Allied Artists, 1953), and again, as Honey Bear, in *The Yellow Tomahawk* (United Artists, 1954).

Moreno found herself in Hollywood at a time when the image of Latins in American film was changing for the worse. Earlier, American moviemakers had used Latin Americans as savage villains and punks in films like *Tony the Greaser* (1911) and *The Greaser's Gauntlet* (1908). In the 1930s, the Latin image in American films was so bad that the Mexican government took steps to ban or censor American films that misrepresented its people.

Because their European market had declined during World War II, Hollywood filmmakers needed to increase their share of the Latin American market, for which they produced American

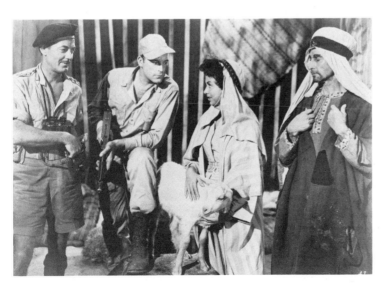

In 1953, Moreno was cast as an Arab woman in Columbia's El Alamein, *a war drama starring Scott Brady (holding machine gun). She later played a Native American in* Fort Vengeance *and* The Yellow Tomahawk.

films dubbed in Spanish. Meanwhile, the United States government wanted to soothe any tension in its relations with the Latin countries in order to counter German propaganda. Consequently, by the early 1940s, Latin characters, music, and dance became extremely popular in the United States. Performers like the Mexican actress Dolores Del Rio, the "Brazilian Bombshell" Carmen Miranda, and the Cuban band leader Desi Arnaz became big hits. In the late 1930s, the actress Lupe Velez became known as "the Mexican spitfire" and the "hot baby of Hollywood." Gossip columnists loved to write shocking stories about Velez's tempestuous life.

Latin stereotypes were firmly set before Moreno came to Hollywood hoping to become a star like Lana Turner or Liz Taylor. During the 1950s, interest in Latin American themes continued, and a few Latin performers, such as the Mexican actor Ricardo Montalban, were given prominent roles. But the filmmakers still wanted their Latin actresses to be dark-eyed firecrackers.

In his book Hispanic Hollywood, *George Hadley-Garcia described the exuberant Carmen Miranda as "a Pan-American potpourri of fruits, colors, hips, pop-eyes, and fractured Eenglish." Known as the Brazilian Bombshell but born in Portugal, Miranda exaggerated Latin stereotypes for comic effect.*

The Mexican film star Dolores Del Rio and the Cuban actor Cesar Romero enjoyed tremendous success during the 1930s and 1940s. Romero sustained his career for some 50 years, appearing in the 1960s television series "Batman" and "Star Trek." During the 1980s, he appeared in the soap opera "Falcon Crest."

Soon after her arrival at MGM, Moreno began her Hollywood social life. Her first date was with Hugh O'Brian, a handsome, up-and-coming leading man. Soon the charming and beautiful Moreno was, according to gossip columnists, one of the most eligible young single women in Hollywood. A *Los Angeles Times* article in 1955 reported that, in an unofficial poll of the Los Angeles police force, Moreno was voted the starlet to whom it would be most fun to serve a traffic ticket. Saucy and witty, Moreno's remarks were often quoted in the press. Once a reporter asked her about the teeth in a necklace she was wearing. She snapped back that they came from old boyfriends. Her antics kept her in the news. For example, once she abandoned a reception line and bounced up to admire the medals of Haile Selassie, the emperor of Ethiopia. "I played the role to the hilt," she later recalls, "because at least it got me attention. It amused and charmed people. 'Isn't she something! What a firecracker!' If that's all I could get then that's what I settled for. There was never a possibility of being anything else in my head, in my perception. The people around didn't help, the society didn't help."

Becoming an adult in Hollywood while playing the role of a sexy Latin starlet took its toll. Moreno, who took her first lover when she was 19, was very naive behind her confident exterior. During her first years of dating, she learned about birth control from her lovers, who were usually older, more experienced men. Plagued by a sense of guilt and inadequacy instilled in her since she was a girl, Moreno had a difficult time feeling good about her own sexuality. When she was 23, she discovered she was pregnant. When she and the man she was involved with decided that Moreno would have an abortion, which at the time was illegal in the United States, he made an appointment with a Beverly Hills doctor who agreed to perform the procedure. That night, back at her apartment, Moreno started to bleed. As the bleeding became heavier and would not stop, Moreno knew she needed help, but she feared that if she went to a hospital she would eventually be sent to jail. Instead, Moreno returned to the doctor, who immediately put her in the hospital and finished the abortion there. Later the doctor admitted to Moreno that she could have bled to death had she not come to him that night.

In her early twenties, Moreno started dating Marlon Brando, a highly acclaimed movie actor then reaching the height of his career and whose attraction to beautiful young Asian and Latin women was well known. Although their relationship was often strained by Brando's interest in other women, they were compatible in many ways. They were both rebellious, had a zany sense of humor, and were concerned about the issues facing minorities. So their relationship grew stronger over the years.

Brando hated publicity about his personal life, and Moreno learned early on not to discuss him with reporters. In 1956, she told a reporter for the *Hollywood News-Citizen*, "I have too much respect and admiration for Marlon to talk about him when I know he doesn't like it," an attitude she maintains to the present day. Nonetheless, Moreno and Brando were regularly followed by the press and, as Moreno once commented, "If we had an argument, my best friends knew about it before I did."

When she was 23 and exasperated with Brando, Moreno started dating George A. Hormel, whom she and others called Geordie, the heir to the Hormel meat-packing fortune. Hormel, who was 26, had decided to pursue a career in music rather than take over his father's business. When Moreno met him, he was in the process of divorcing his first wife, the dancer Leslie Caron. Moreno had a deep crush on this sensitive, talented, glamorous young man. At the time, she was living with a roommate at the Hollywood Studio Club, a women's residence run by the YWCA.

After they had been dating for about five months, Moreno and Hormel became embroiled in a drug scandal. One evening, Moreno was sleeping on the couch at Hormel's home, waiting for him to return after his show at a Los Angeles nightclub. Unknown to Hormel, someone Hormel had thought was a loyal friend, bass player Robert "Iggy" Shevak, had turned informer for the police. Shevak told the police that Hormel was smoking marijuana and that they would find a stash of rolled marijuana, or joints, in his car behind the sun visor. The police tailed Hormel's Packard as he drove home after the club closed and arrested him at his home after finding the marijuana.

Moreno and George A. Hormel attend a Hollywood social affair in 1954. Hormel, a pianist and heir to the Hormel meat-packing fortune, decided against running his father's business and instead pursued a career in music. His and Moreno's much-publicized affair lasted five months.

The police took him into the house, found Moreno asleep, and told him to "wake up Sleeping Beauty." Moreno woke up to see Hormel standing between two undercover detectives. One grabbed her overnight bag and, without explanation, started going through it. Furious at this unexplained invasion of privacy, and uncertain who these intruders were, Moreno summoned all of her strength and kicked the man in the shin. She then slugged him in the stomach so hard that he threatened to file charges against her for impeding an investigation.

Newspapers sizzled with stories about the "ham king" and Hollywood's "sexy pixy." The press wanted to know what was in Moreno's overnight bag. Moreno denied that she or Hormel ever smoked marijuana, and she has always insisted that Hormel was framed. She told one reporter for the *New York Daily News*, "I didn't strike the officer. I just pushed him in the stomach. But why didn't he show a badge or something?" Later in court she apologized to the officers. They in turn dropped the charges against her and admitted that her bag contained only personal items.

Moreno's roommate, Louise Martinson, strongly advised a terrified and confused Moreno to stay away from Hormel. She thought their phone might be tapped. The studio, concerned that the publicity could make one of their starlets look bad, gave her lessons about press conferences. Although she offered to testify on Hormel's behalf, she was never with him again, a decision that Moreno recalls regretfully because she knew she had abandoned someone she really cared for when he was in need. Eventually, the charges against Hormel were dropped.

While doggedly working her way through television fare, unemployment lines, and more B movies such as *Ma and Pa Kettle on Vacation*, Moreno auditioned for another seemingly insignificant part in 1954. Little did she know that this small role would lead to opportunities she still only dreamed about. She was to perform with Ray Bolger, who was making a pilot for a proposed series called "The Ray Bolger Show." Moreno was to be his dancing partner. During that time, *Life* magazine had reporters in Hollywood to cover the boom in a new phenomenon, the television series. The

Moreno testifies on behalf of the defendant, George Hormel, who was arrested and tried on charges of drug possession in 1954. The charges were later dropped.

Life editors saw Moreno in several of Bolger's publicity photos, thought she was attractive, and wanted to know who she was. They sent reporters to interview Moreno for a story and assigned Lewis Dean to photograph her. Moreno was amazed by this surprising turn of events. *Life* had a tremendous circulation and influence. When the editors let her know they were considering her for the cover, she could barely believe it was true. She asked the editors what could prevent her from being on the cover, and they responded, "If Eisenhower gets the flu."

President Eisenhower must have remained in good health, because the cover of *Life*, a saucy portrait of Moreno with parted lips and a bare shoulder hit the newsstands in March 1954 and was an enormous success with the public. The accompanying story included photos of her in various roles. Of course, she was overjoyed when the issue was published.

That month, Moreno was in Mexico filming *Garden of Evil* (20th Century Fox, 1954), which starred Gary Cooper, Susan Hayward, and Richard Widmark. The head of 20th Century Fox, Darryl Zanuck, saw the *Life* cover as well as other newsphotos that showed Moreno singing and flirting with Gary Cooper. He reportedly responded, "Hot number. Find out who she is and if she can speak English." Soon after, Fox signed Moreno to a seven-year contract, and her star was once more on the rise.

In 1954, Moreno signed a seven-year deal with 20th Century Fox and proceeded to make a number of major motion pictures. Here she is on the set of Untamed, *an adventure movie filmed in South Africa and released in 1955.*

CHAPTER FIVE

The Oscar and After

In no way did signing with Fox make Moreno an instant movie star. It quickly became apparent that she still had a long, hard climb ahead of her. Fox first cast her in *Untamed* (1955), an adventure film set in South Africa. Though she was given a larger part than in her previous films, Moreno was still cast, as one *New York Post* critic wrote, as "a fiery love machine." The same writer called on the powers at Fox to give Moreno a break and let her play a substantial role. But the studio had other ideas.

Soon after Moreno signed with Fox, the publicity department sent out press packets on Moreno, promoting her as their Latina sex kitten, and set up interviews for her with Hollywood columnists. Moreno played her role for the press very well. In one article, the writer called her a "Puerto Rican firecracker" and noted that "when she was signed by 20th Century Fox, she couldn't wait for the studio publicity to send out pictures, so she mailed copies of pin-up shots personally to columnists and editors." Other articles reported on her alleged 24-hour use of perfume (even in bed), her temper, her love of earrings and high-heeled shoes with straps, and her stuffed dog named Bunny. Moreno told one Hollywood reporter, "I generally play bad women. But I'm not really bad. Like in *Untamed*, I'm only bad because my boyfriend won't have me and makes me bad."

Once again Fox cast Moreno as poor, brown-skinned, barefooted, hot-blooded Native American maiden, named Ula, who loses her man to the white leading lady played by Rhonda Fleming. In this western, *Seven Cities of Gold* (1955), Moreno was in a pathetic scene near the end of the movie when her character found out she had been jilted by the leading man, played by Richard Egan. Moreno asked him, "Why joo no luv Ula no more?" After he answered, she took two steps back and fell off a 100-foot cliff. Moreno often refers to that scene as a classic of the "Yonkee peeg" school of acting and script writing.

Moreno's prospects brightened when she appeared in *The Lieutenant Wore Skirts* (1955). This was her first opportunity to show her natural ability to do comedy. At one point in the movie, she did a takeoff of Marilyn Monroe, wearing a blond wig and loads of padding. And in this film she was cast as an ordinary American with a costume that included shoes.

The most acclaimed film that Moreno made for Fox during the 1950s was The King and I, *which starred Yul Brynner and Deborah Kerr. In this scene from the movie, Moreno, as Tuptim the Asian princess, kneels before her master, the king of Siam.*

Although being cast as Tuptim in the film version of *The King and I* in 1956 meant she was once again playing a dark-eyed foreigner, Moreno was more than ready to take the part. The film version of the hit musical, starring Yul Brynner and Deborah Kerr, was her first substantial film role. The studio bosses did not actually think of Moreno for the part; she got it inadvertently. Because she was under contract to Fox, she was asked to help screen-test the men being considered for Tuptim's love interest. When two actresses scheduled to do the role backed out, one after the other, the casting director decided to give Moreno the part. In the movie business, breaks such as these come, if at all, once in a lifetime.

As Tuptim the Asian princess, Moreno had a significant part in *The King and I.* She sang all her own songs, rather than following common practice and having another person dub them, and narrated the film's famous ballet sequence, which was choreographed by Jerome Robbins. Moreno was also thrilled at the chance to wear interesting costumes. "Usually," she told a reporter only half jokingly, "I go through a movie in buckskin and tattered rags."

Jerome Robbins remembered Moreno a year later when he began the choreography for Leonard Bernstein's new Broadway musical, *West Side Story.* He asked Moreno to audition for the ingenue lead, Maria, but she decided not to, partly because she wanted to focus on her film career and partly because she was afraid to go back on stage. She had recently been dismissed after one week of rehearsals from a theater production of Tennessee Williams's *Camino Real* when Williams said he did not like her voice and demanded that the director replace her. *West Side Story* had a hugely successful run on Broadway, and Moreno regretted her decision not to audition.

After *The King and I,* Moreno got a part in the film operetta *The Vagabond King* (1956). She played a tavern wench named Hugette. Her last film for Fox was *The Deerslayer* (1957). Then, without explanation, the studio let her contract lapse, and once again Moreno, now 25, had to start over. After a three-year period without making a movie, Moreno was cast in *This Rebel Breed* (1960).

An ecstatic Moreno, as the tavern wench Hugette, dances wildly on a tabletop in The Vagabond King, *a film operetta released in 1956. The following year she appeared in* The Deerslayer, *and in 1960 she was cast in* This Rebel Breed.

Moreno faced this frustration and disappointment with the help of her therapist, Dr. Murray Korngold, with whom she worked for eight years. A friend of hers observed that Moreno was unusually jolly during this period, and Moreno agrees, believing that what she was doing was turning on the charm in order to hide her real feelings. She was still struggling with deeply rooted anxieties and fears that had remained with her from childhood. Also, even though on the surface it appeared not to bother her, Moreno resented being told that her audition was fine but that what was needed was someone who looked more like a "real American," someone like Mitzi Gaynor.

Going to Dr. Korngold was not easy for Moreno. She was nervous and afraid. Later she recalled, "I really didn't know how hard it was going to be, and I didn't know how wonderful it was going to be—hard because I had to face hard truths, and wonderful because every step I took was not only earned but cause for jubilation. Self-esteem begins to build when you're able to understand what you're doing that's harmful to your life and begin to do something about it. And that takes a while."

Moreno continued her rounds of auditions, but she was becoming more selective, turning down parts she considered offensive. For example, she refused a television role as a young Eurasian woman who could only speak a few words of pidgin English. Moreno's response, after reading the script, was that it did not call for an actress but "a female body filled with formaldehyde."

Between auditions and unemployment checks, Moreno enrolled in a philosophy course at the University of California at Los Angeles and began taking acting classes. Although strong film roles were hard to come by, she was determined to keep working and turned her attention to the theater.

Moreno built a successful career in summer stock and regional theatre, traveling from La Jolla, California, to Seattle, Washington, and even across the country. She found theater producers and directors to be more imaginative and less limited by prejudice than their Hollywood counterparts. They invited her to audition for many interesting and diverse roles. She played Lola in *Damn Yankees*, Annie Sullivan in *The Miracle Worker*, Sally Bowles in *I Am a Camera*, Adelaide in *Guys and Dolls*, and other rich characters.

During the late 1950s and early 1960s, Moreno became increasingly involved in summer stock and regional theatre. She performed in productions of Damn Yankees, The Miracle Worker, I Am a Camera, *and* Guys and Dolls, *among others.*

Although she enjoyed performing on stage, Moreno never let go of her dream of being a film star. The extensive touring began to take its toll, and her frustration began to build. Then she had a brush with tragedy.

On February 13, 1960, she and Brando were driving in a storm when his sports car went out of control and crashed. Moreno's face was badly cut, and she was rushed to the hospital. When she saw a troop of reporters there to meet them, Moreno went into a fury of screaming and tried to chase them away. The stories and pictures in the papers the next day, showing an enraged Moreno, her head wrapped in bandages, reinforced the public image of her as a hot-tempered Latina. Later that year, when Moreno and Brando were spotted by reporters and photographers at a Hollywood theater opening, the actor glowered at the paparazzi and made an insulting gesture at them. Undaunted, the photographers snapped photos of the two celebrities, and the next day Brando was pictured in the press holding his hand up to the camera, his middle finger air-brushed out.

Despite Moreno's growing personal sadness, her career started to regain its sparkle. By the fall of 1960, she was working in two films, *Summer and Smoke* (Paramount 1961), a film adaptation of an acclaimed Tennessee Williams play starring Geraldine Page, and *West Side Story*, released in 1961 by United Artists.

When she had arrived for the audition for *West Side Story*, Moreno had been exhausted from a long day of shooting another television show. There were five other actresses up for the role of Anita. Even though Jerome Robbins, the choreographer for the film, had requested that she audition for the role, Moreno was sure she would not get it.

West Side Story is based on Shakespeare's *Romeo and Juliet*, a tale of two lovers who struggled desperately to be together in a society that made their union impossible. *West Side Story* takes place in the working-class neighborhoods of New York City in the 1950s. The lovers, Tony and Maria, played by Richard Beymer and Natalie Wood, were from rival street gangs, the Jets and the Sharks, and their ill-fated affair ended in tragedy.

Moreno plays the role of Anita in West Side Story. *Based on William Shakespeare's* Romeo and Juliet, West Side Story *was directed by Robert Wise. Leonard Bernstein wrote the score, and Jerome Robbins choreographed the dance sequences.*

For the audition, the director, Robert Wise, asked Moreno to do a scene where Anita is nearly raped in a drugstore, and he read the lines of one of the characters, which were racial slurs aimed at Moreno's character. When she heard the lines and the insulting language they contained—"Ya lyin' Spic," "Gold Tooth," "Garlic Breath," "Pierced Ear,"—Moreno was thrown back to her childhood when she used to hear such taunts on her way to school. Once the reading was over, she ran out of the room, collapsed on a couch, and wept.

Moreno got the part. However, the production suffered a setback in September when Moreno showed up for work with one of her hands and wrists bandaged. The newspapers reported an odd story that she said she had been shadowboxing with her roommate when she accidentally put her hand through a window. Many people believed, however, that Rita had attempted to take her own life.

Moreno earned the director's respect for her inventiveness, range, and professionalism. Sometimes she arrived on the set of *West Side Story* after many hours of shooting *Summer and Smoke,* but she never complained about being tired. In fact she often entertained the crew during her hours off camera by performing the role of a no-talent Puerto Rican singer who was forever auditioning for the musical *Gypsy*, singing "Everything's Coming Up Roses" in an extremely exaggerated Spanish accent.

Although the studio bosses called Moreno "opinionated" and "stubborn," especially when they wanted her to do more revealing interviews and publicity appearances, she was always extremely cooperative with directors and producers. "I wasn't difficult ever," Moreno recalls. "I was the most passive person on earth. For the most part I was pathetically malleable. It's really what kept me from being a better actress. In order to be an actor or actress of some breadth and some size, you have to have a measure of independence: 'This is how I see this role. This is what I think is right.' I never had the guts to do that with acting roles. When I look at *The King and I*, I feel so bad. A lot of my early work was insipid."

Moreno continued to see a lot of Brando, but their relationship seemed to consist of one upsetting episode after another. The tabloids were dripping with gossip about Brando's romantic escapades, and the custody fight with his former wife over their son made regular headlines. Brando, several years older than Moreno, once broke up with her for mentioning his name in an interview. She never talked to the press about him again. But their complex and passionate relationship had its final crisis in April 1961.

Moreno was visiting Brando regularly on the set of *Mutiny on the Bounty* but suddenly stopped coming. On April 10, the press reported that Brando had testified in his custody trial that he had secretly married one of his old girlfriends, Movita, a Mexican film actress, and they had an 11-month-old son. Newspapers reported that Moreno visited the set the very next day. Then, on April 19, 1961, at about one in the afternoon, Moreno, 29 years old and filled with despair about her dead-end relationship with Brando and her stalled career, drove to Brando's house. There, in his living room, she swallowed a handful of sleeping pills. Fortunately, Brando's longtime secretary was there and immediately called St. John's Hospital in Santa Monica. As Moreno lost consciousness, a doctor arrived at the Brando home and called an ambulance. In the emergency room, the doctors found no reflexes. But Moreno survived. A few days later, a roommate picked her up at the hospital, helped her avoid a siege of reporters, and drove her to their Laurel Canyon home.

Unfortunately, at the time when she was feeling so depressed, a doctor had prescribed the drug phenobarbital to treat her hyperthyroid condition. He never cautioned her that this medicine could make her depression worse. Moreno eventually stopped taking the drug as her life came back into focus.

Moreno used this terrifying experience to grow in self-esteem and self-knowledge. She realized that she was trying to do away with her life when all she really wanted to do away with was the terrible emotional pain over her relationships, her career, and her feelings of inadequacy left over from her childhood. Years later, looking back on her experience, she counseled that anyone who feels that wretched must somehow remember that life will change. "As bad as it feels and as permanent as that emotional pain feels at the time, it does change. Time simply changes things. It changes perception, it even changes the problem."

When she got home from the hospital, Moreno took stock of her life. She continued taking acting classes and watched *West Side Story* become a huge hit. She marched in a demonstration against nuclear weapons. She dreamed more and more often about Puerto Rico and her Hispanic roots. In January 1962, Moreno donated $1,000 toward an acting scholarship at the University of Puerto Rico and returned to the island to deliver her gift. She was received with much fanfare and pride.

Shortly after returning to Los Angeles, Moreno was cast as a Filipino guerrilla in another action-packed B movie, *To Be a Man*, starring Van Heflin. Moreno packed her bags and boarded a plane for Manila, the capital of the Philippines.

Moreno had simply laughed when her friends said she might be nominated for an Academy Award for her work in *West Side Story*.

Moreno in To Be a Man, *filmed on location in the Philippines. For the bathing scene, which she had planned to do in the nude, Moreno wore a loosely fitting cotton bathing gown so as not to offend the Filipino vice president, who had voiced objections to the scene as originally conceived.*

None of the young actors in the film ever dared to dream that it would be the success that it ultimately was.

But the unbelievable came true. Moreno was nominated for an Oscar as Best Supporting Actress. Sweating in the steamy Philippine jungle working on a film she hated, Moreno made up her mind to go to the awards ceremony. If there was even a breath of a chance that she would win, she wanted to be there.

At first the director said he would not let her go, but eventually Moreno worked out an arrangement that allowed her to be gone for three days. She bought a plane ticket and then had a gown made by a Filipino seamstress. It was fashioned from obi fabric, a material used to make the sashes worn with oriental kimonos. The dress cost about $100, which at the time was a strain on Moreno's budget; but, she reasoned, how often is one nominated for an Academy Award?

As she packed her bag and boarded the plane, Moreno never thought she could really win. Judy Garland, who was hospitalized at the time, was also nominated for Best Supporting Actress, and cameras were set up next to her bed in case she won. Moreover, with international time changes and the many fueling stops, the flight each way took about 24 hours. That meant Moreno would have two days of travel and only one day in Los Angeles. Still Moreno was determined to be there.

When she finally arrived at her mother's home, Moreno had only a few hours to rest and get ready before she had to leave for the awards ceremony. United Artists, with some hesitation, agreed to pay for a limousine to pick up Moreno and George Chakiris, who was nominated for Best Supporting Actor for his role in *West Side Story.* All the way to the ceremony at the Santa Monica Civic Auditorium, Chakiris and Moreno joked and laughed, making up sour grapes speeches in case they lost.

That evening, April 9, 1962, *West Side Story* swept the awards, earning 10 Oscars. The film's first award that evening went to Chakiris. Later, Moreno's name was pulled from the envelope and announced as the winner of the award for Best Supporting Actress.

Moreno holds her Oscar for Best Supporting Actress, which she received in 1962 for her performance in West Side Story. *With her are (from left) George Chakiris, who won Best Supporting Actor for his performance in* West Side Story, *Greer Garson, and Maximilian Schell.*

Moreno was overwhelmed. Her mother, who was sitting right behind her, messed up her hair and hugged and shook her hard. Then time went into slow motion. Moreno thought to herself as she headed for the stage that she must not run. She always hated seeing people run up for their awards. As she started up the stairs, she remembered that she had promised herself that, if she won, she would not thank anyone. She thought, "I got this for my performance, not because the academy is doing me a great favor." She was not going to make a phony acceptance speech; instead she burst into tears.

Standing on the stage that evening, Moreno made history as the first Hispanic woman ever to receive an Oscar. A few days later, the Puerto Rican legislature voted to fund a commemorative plaque honoring Moreno as the first Puerto Rican to win an Oscar.

Chakiris and Moreno danced and partied all night, bathing in as much glory as possible. Regretfully, the next morning, she had to board a plane for the grueling trip back to Manila. She wanted to remain in Los Angeles and be congratulated, receive flowers, give interviews and generally bask in the praise she deserved. Instead, it was back to work.

After the completion of *To Be a Man*, Moreno stayed on to do some television programs in Manila before flying home. She anticipated having to deal with the intense pressure of being an Oscar winner, but when she got back she seemed to have what one gossip columnist called the "Oscar's Curse," noting that many performers see their careers stall after winning the film industry's top award. In May, Moreno gave a list to a *Los Angeles Times* reporter of all the offers she had received to date. They included magazines wanting to interview her or write her life story if she would talk about Marlon Brando; seven chances to star in independently produced films, though three were contingent on her helping with the financing; product endorsements for things such as margarine and lipstick; and six written marriage proposals from strangers. Eventually, she agreed to star in a production of *Damn Yankees* in Dayton, Ohio.

Moreno marches with others through downtown Los Angeles on August 9, 1963, to protest the city's failure to effectively integrate its school system. During the 1960s, she became increasingly active in politics and often spoke out on civil rights issues.

When Moreno was cast as a camp follower in the Allied Artists film *Cry of Battle* (1963), her frustration and her doubts about the life she had chosen in Hollywood peaked. On July 30, 1962, her letter to the editor appeared in *Daily Variety*, taking the legendary actress Bette Davis to task for her published comments critical of the civil rights movement. In her letter, Moreno denied that Davis spoke for their profession, and wrote, "So long as any American citizen or group of citizens is deprived of dignity and freedom, then my own freedom and sense of personal dignity are also inevitably threatened." She concluded, "Hollywood Jim Crowism must end now in all its aspects."

With the studios in the United States offering very little of interest, Moreno considered relocating to London, which at the time had a flourishing theater scene. She discussed the matter with her mother and decided to make the move. She gave notice to her roommates, said good-bye to her therapist, and packed her bags. In September 1963 the announcement in the *Los Angeles Times* read "Rita Moreno to live in London where she will make her permanent home." A very new and interesting chapter in Moreno's life was about to begin.

Moreno and her husband, Leonard Gordon, on their wedding day, June 18, 1965, at New York's City Hall. They were introduced by a mutual friend, Leah Schaefer.

CHAPTER SIX

In Excellent Company

Moreno left her despair behind her and turned her attention to working on the London stage. Only two months after her arrival in England, U.S. president John Kennedy was assassinated in Dallas, Texas, on November 22, 1963. Moreno, like countless people in the United States and around the world, was shocked and dismayed. Despite her excitement at living in a glamorous city like London, the tragedy left her with a lingering desire to be back in the United States.

Hal Prince, a well-known theater director, had other ideas for Moreno, however. He was directing *She Loves Me*, an American musical for the Lyric Theatre in London's West End, which is like New York's Broadway theater district. During rehearsals, the actress playing Ilona Ritter, an important role in the play, became ill. Prince knew that Moreno was living in London and felt that she was perfect for the part. Of course Moreno wanted it. She had come to London to act. Prince hired her, and they went to work.

Soon, however, British Equity, the actors' union, strenuously objected to Moreno's taking the part. The union's rules required that British productions use British actors. Prince was irate. Opening night was very close, and he did not want to let Moreno go. He threatened to close the show if they forced him to fire her. Realizing that if he did so, all the British actors in the cast would lose their jobs, the union relented. *She Loves Me* opened on April 29, 1964, and Moreno received rave reviews from the London critics.

But the writing was on the wall. When she chose to move to England in order to leave behind Hollywood's pettiness and prejudices, Moreno had not expected to be stymied by the strict union rules that protected British actors. Hal Prince, who enjoyed working with Moreno, provided a solution. He called her from New York and offered her a part in a new Lorraine Hansberry play, *The Sign in Sidney Brustein's Window*, which he was going to direct. Moreno gladly accepted, packed again, and moved back to New York in 1964 to play Iris Parodus Brustein at the Longacre Theatre.

This play about Greenwich Village life opened in October, developed a big following, and ran for a remarkable 101 perfor-

Moreno and her costar, Gabriel Dell, clown around prior to the opening of Lorraine Hansberry's Sign in Sidney Brustein's Window, *at New York's Longacre Theatre. The play was a great success, running for 101 performances, and Moreno's performance received high critical praise.*

mances. Relieved to be rid of Hollywood typecasting, Moreno was grateful that in the theater she was allowed to use her acting skills to create a character who was not a Latina. Once back in New York, Moreno also made time to work briefly for the Southern Christian Leadership Conference in support of a civil rights campaign led by Dr. Martin Luther King, Jr.

During the Christmas holiday season in 1964, Leah Schaefer, a psychotherapist and close friend of Moreno's, asked Rita if she might be interested in meeting a man she was sure Rita would find interesting, a doctor named Leonard Gordon. Moreno agreed to go on a double date, and Schaefer set it up.

Their first evening together was so enjoyable that Lenny, an internist with a specialty in cardiology, invited Rita to a New Year's Eve party. She accepted and asked him to meet her after the show at the Longacre. Lenny was puzzled at the late hour and wondered if perhaps the reason for it was that Rita had earlier made a date to see the show, probably with another man. But he decided to meet Rita as she requested. He went to the Longacre well before the show was over and waited out front in the cold. As the playgoers emerged from the theater, Rita was nowhere in sight. Confused and thinking he might have been stood up, he asked an usher to check the women's restroom. No Rita.

Meanwhile, Moreno was backstage in her dressing room fuming. She could not believe she would be stood up on New Year's Eve! Gordon was upset too. What could have happened? It occurred to him that he might be at the wrong theater. He hurried outside to check the marquee. There he read in lights "Starring Rita Moreno." He hurried backstage, found an angry Moreno, apologized, and asked, "Are you *the* Rita Moreno?" Although Lenny knew she was an actress, it had not occurred to him that she was Rita Moreno the celebrity. Lenny was somewhat embarrassed, Rita was charmed, and the evening was delightful for both of them.

On June 18, 1965, Rita Moreno, who was 33, married Lenny Gordon, who was 45. It was her first marriage and his second.

Twenty friends and relatives joined them for a simple ceremony performed by the New York State Supreme Court Justice Samuel M. Gold in his chambers at City Hall. Afterward they all went out for a Chinese dinner. After dinner, Leah Schaefer quipped, "The trouble with getting married and then eating a Chinese dinner is that three hours later you want to get married again!"

Her marriage to Lenny Gordon began a long and fruitful partnership that Moreno often credits for providing the balance she had sought for so long. Both Rita and Lenny came from very poor families and grew up in ethnic communities, and the similarities in their backgrounds helped them to understand each other's motivations and fears. Moreover, Lenny's dry sense of humor and orderly mind combined with Rita's drive and expressiveness to create a stable but dynamic relationship. A reporter for *Cue* magazine once noted that, asked if he could prescribe something inexpensive and nonaddictive that would keep a person high without a hangover, Lenny replied, "Sure. Marry Rita."

In 1967, Moreno gave birth to a daughter, Fernanda Luisa, her only child. With the arrival of their new baby, Moreno and Gordon began to spend more time outside the city, at a house in Upstate New York, where they concentrated not only on parenting but also on gardening.

In 1967, Moreno gave birth to a daughter, Fernanda Luisa, whom she and Lenny nicknamed Nandy. Although both Rita and Lenny wanted to have more children, they never did. Soon after Nandy's birth, they started spending most weekends at a country house in Upstate New York. One day they stood together in their vegetable garden laughing at themselves—a poor Puerto Rican girl from el barrio and a poor Jewish kid from the Bronx, raising their first tomato.

Moreno was not working when Fernanda was born, so she was able to focus nearly all of her attention on the baby. She once recalled that "I never knew I could love any human being so much. I didn't have a clue so much good stuff was stored up inside me." Lenny was an attentive and involved parent, happily washing dishes, changing diapers, or whatever needed to be done. "Nandy," recalls Moreno, "was the most wanted baby on earth, a pure, unadulterated joy. That's why I feel so strongly about choice." Moreno is outspoken about her support of reproductive choice for women and was profiled in a book of interviews about women and men who have had experience with abortion.

Lenny continued to maintain his practice until Nandy was about three years old. He suffered from congenital heart problems that became so serious that he was forced to retire. He turned his attention to caring for Nandy and learning more about show business, eventually becoming Moreno's manager.

On April 4, 1968, America was stunned by the assassination of Dr. Martin Luther King, Jr. Although the civil rights movement had made great strides since the 1950s, the issues of racial equality and equal opportunity were far from resolved when Dr. King was murdered. In Hollywood, where for a time there had been signs that a more enlightened attitude was taking hold, Latin Americans were now increasingly portrayed as inherently violent people and basically inept or even stupid. Hispanic film actors, even those who had achieved stardom in the 1950s and early 1960s like Fernando Lamas, Ricardo Montalban, and Katy Jurado, again found them-

Moreno, as Serafina, prepares to take a swat at Alan Nixon in the 1968 production of Tennessee Williams's Rose Tattoo, *at the Ivanhoe Theater in Chicago. The Chicago theater critics awarded her the prestigious Joseph Jefferson Award for her performance in the play.*

selves cast in derogatory roles such as those of bandits and prostitutes, or not cast at all. In response to this return to the worst kind of stereotyping, Montalban, in 1970, founded Nosotros (Us), an organization devoted to promoting positive change for Hispanics in the American film industry.

In 1968, Moreno was cast as Serafina in a production of Tennessee Williams's play *The Rose Tattoo,* at the Ivanhoe Theater in Chicago. Not only did she receive standing ovations for her performance, but she was presented with the prestigious Joseph Jefferson Award given by the Chicago theater critics. Today, Moreno smiles at the irony of her great success in a play written by a man who had once fired her from his cast.

Moreno never lost her love for film acting, and she made every effort to land new film roles. But she had trouble finding work. A devoted performer, she worked wherever she could, not limiting herself to one medium. One day Marlon Brando, with whom she remained close friends, called to tell her about a new movie he was going to make. Then he asked her if she would like a part in it. "What a question!" Moreno responded, "Of course!"

In 1968, Moreno flew to Paris for the filming, and was joined later by Lenny and Nandy, who was two years old. This was the first film Moreno had made since 1963. The movie, *The Night of the Following Day* (Universal, 1969), was unsuccessful, but Moreno received favorable reviews, including praise from the influential film critic for the *New Yorker*, Pauline Kael, who wrote that she gave "an expert and stylized performance."

In 1969, Moreno was offered two more film roles. She joined James Garner in a detective film, *Marlowe* (1969), for MGM. The filming required that she live in Los Angeles for the first time in

Moreno and Marlon Brando in the 1969 Universal Pictures release The Night of the Following Day. *Although the film was not well received, Moreno's performance was praised by such demanding critics as Pauline Kael of the* New Yorker.

Moreno and Alan Arkin in Popi, *which was filmed on location in New York City. The 1969 comedy took a lighthearted look at the trials and tribulations of Puerto Rican immigrants in East Harlem.*

six years. She and her family rented a large house in Beverly Hills that was once owned by the actress Rhonda Fleming. During this short stay, both Lenny and Rita were reminded about the difficult realities of the Hollywood film industry but also discovered that the milder weather was much better for Lenny's serious heart condition.

That year, Moreno took a small role as Alan Arkin's Puerto Rican girlfriend in a much praised performance in the comedy *Popi* (United Artists, 1969), which was set in East Harlem. Although *Popi* was filmed in New York, Moreno and her family visited Hollywood for the opening night celebration. In 1971, Moreno returned to Hollywood again to play a small but intense and highly regarded role as a prostitute in Jules Feiffer's dark comedy, *Carnal Knowledge* (Avco-Embassy, 1971).

In 1970, Moreno went back to work on the New York stage, playing the role of Sharon Falconer in a short-lived production of the musical *Gantry*. Later that year, she took over for Linda Lavin as the lead in *The Last of the Red Hot Lovers*, a long-running hit comedy by Neil Simon.

Moreno and her daughter, Fernanda (far right) on the set of the children's television show "The Electric Company" in 1971. The following year, the soundtrack recording made by the show's cast won a Grammy for Best Recording for Children.

The following year, Moreno's flair for comedy, and her love of zany characters and clowning around, found perfect expression when she was invited to join the cast of "The Electric Company." The producers of "Sesame Street," the Children's Television Workshop, wanted to create a program aimed at helping 7-to-10-year-olds improve their reading. They were determined to form a multiracial ensemble of actors who would play numerous characters for the fast-paced, vaudeville-style episodes. Moreno, the only Hispanic in the cast during the first season, joined Bill Cosby and Morgan Freeman, among others, to inaugurate "The Electric Company," broadcast on PBS throughout the United States.

Moreno decided to join "The Electric Company" and stayed with the show for five out of its six seasons for several reasons. As she told a *TV Guide* interviewer, "I am Latin and know what it is to feel alone and ignored because you are different. When you are ignored, you have lost your sense of identity. So I can be the Latin on this show and my presence there can tell a lot of children and some adults, 'Yes, we do exist, we have value.'" In addition, her apartment was conveniently located only a couple of blocks from the studio, so she could walk to work and even go home to be with Nandy at lunch or have Nandy visit her on the set. She went to the studio about three times a week to tape her part of the show.

The cast of "The Electric Company" got along very well and had a great time making the show. Moreno remembers wanting to laugh so badly during some of the skits that her eyes watered and she bit her lip. She loved going to work. On a typical day, she would arrive at the studio about 9:00 A.M. and immediately go into the makeup room, where the other cast members were also having their makeup and hair done. While they were worked on, the cast started discussing the scripts and exchanging ideas about how they would do their skits. Next, Moreno and the others went to wardrobe. The actors were encouraged to make suggestions about their makeup and costumes. Sometimes a prop or a costume change, like the addition of a beauty mark or a fancy frill, would suggest a new way of doing a character.

Next, Moreno went to the set for the first skit. The actors worked as an ensemble, meaning that no one was given more important roles than anyone else. Each actor played many characters. Moreno's favorites, and ones she is often remembered for, were Otto, the dictatorial and flustered movie director, and Pandore, a spoiled little brat with blond curls. On the set, the actors would usually rehearse once, at most twice, and then go right into their performance with the cameras rolling. They had to work fast and stay in tune with one another. Then they would go back to wardrobe and makeup to change quickly for the next scene. By 5:00 P.M., the day's shoot would be finished. Before everyone left, they were given another script to take home to read. It took about six months of work to tape each season's shows.

"The Electric Company" was an immediate success, but Bill Cosby decided to leave the show for other projects. Moreno convinced the producers to hire a Hispanic to replace Cosby. After a series of auditions, the cast and directors joined in choosing Luis Avalos, a young Cuban actor who had grown up in New York. Avalos recalls, "When I got on the show, the first thing I had to do was tell Rita how, as a young teenager, I remembered watching her get the Oscar for *West Side Story*. I was so emotional about it because there she was, a Hispanic woman, getting that award."

On Avalos's first day working on the set, the director lined up the cast, one in front of the other with Moreno first in line, to shoot a sequence that would be used to open every show. Avalos assumed, since he was still in a rabbit costume from the previous skit and because he was the newest cast member, that he should go to the end of the line. He has never forgotten that Moreno pulled him over and placed him directly in front of her, a remarkably generous gesture for an actor. She told him bluntly that this was where he belonged and to never forget that he was important. From that moment on, Avalos felt accepted by the cast and free to take risks as he created his characters. He and Moreno became good friends, and she helped him with his career whenever she could. Avalos later said, "Rita is a very hardworking, generous woman. She demands the best of herself and of the people she works with."

In 1972, a soundtrack recording by the "Electric Company" cast won a Grammy, which is like the Oscar for the recording industry, for Best Recording for Children. There is an old saying that "life begins at 40." For Moreno, now 40, the future was looking brighter than ever.

Moreno as Googie Gomez on the set of The Ritz, *which opened on Broadway in 1975. The character, Moreno's own creation, was a spoof on the many exaggerated Latin stereotypes that had for decades found their way into American film and theater.*

CHAPTER SEVEN

Doin' Googie Gomez

In 1975, a lively moment from Moreno's past came back, not to haunt her but to bring a wonderful reward. Years before, in 1961, when she was filming *West Side Story*, Moreno would entertain the cast and crew as Googie Gomez, a Puerto Rican singer who was absolutely untalented, bighearted, and unstoppably ambitious. Googie was always auditioning for truck and bus companies touring the musical *Gypsy*, singing "Everything's Coming Up Roses" in an extremely exaggerated Spanish accent. For Moreno, Googie was a satire of the stereotypical way so many people saw Hispanics. Her audience of actors, grips, wardrobe ladies, and hairdressers loved her character and often called for Moreno to sing "Roses" again.

Over the years, when Moreno attended a party, inevitably people would beg her to sing "Roses." One evening, Moreno went to a birthday party for James Coco, whom she played opposite in *The Last of the Red Hot Lovers*. Inevitably, Coco asked Moreno to sing "Roses," and she agreed; but, she said, first Googie wanted to give him an acting lesson. As Googie, Moreno recited the Player King's speech from *Hamlet* in fractured English before breaking into her raucous version of "Everything's Coming Up Roses." A guest at the party, playwright Terrance McNally, was crazy about the character Moreno had invented. He told her that night that he was going to write a play for Googie. Moreno thought that was great, but she did not expect it to really happen. Nevertheless, she answered in the voice of her character, "Joo write, I play!"

Meanwhile, in addition to performing in "The Electric Company," in March 1973, Moreno took the part of a shoplifter in a production of Sidney Kingsley's *Detective Story* in Philadelphia. The production was intended for Broadway but was not successful enough to make it there. During the 1973–74 theater season, Moreno played Staff Nurse Norton in Peter Nichol's *The National Health* at the Long Wharf Theatre in New Haven, Connecticut. Early in 1974, Lenny Gordon happened to meet James Coco while they were both walking on Broadway in New York. Coco asked Gordon if he had read the script. Gordon asked him what script he was talking about. Mysteriously, Coco would only say that a copy was on its way. Moreno received a script in the mail from McNally a few days later. It was called *The Tubs* and featured Googie Gomez, the Puerto Rican singer Moreno had created.

Soon, McNally invited Rita and Lenny over to the Yale Repertory Theatre, also in New Haven, to see a play-in-progress performance of McNally's farce set in a gay bathhouse. Moreno was amazed to see her character living in a full-length play, though she felt uncomfortable seeing another actress trying to play the character she had created. She could not wait to do Googie Gomez herself.

McNally's play, renamed *The Ritz*, opened on Broadway at the Longacre Theatre in 1975 with Moreno in the role of Googie Gomez. For Moreno, Googie was not only a hilarious exaggeration of a stereotypical Latina singer, she was a takeoff on bad but earnest performers everywhere. *The Ritz*, and especially Moreno, became a smash hit. Googie wiggled, cursed, and stormed through her song-

and-dance numbers in a barrage of fractured English. When questioned by a *New York Times* reporter if her character might offend Hispanics, Moreno said, "By playing Googie, I'm thumbing my nose at all those Hollywood writers responsible for lines like 'Yankee peeg, you rape my seester, I keel you!' Those writers were serious and Terrance is not. All the characters in *The Ritz* are outrageous caricatures and that's how I play Googie, outrageously!"

The Ritz, with its remarkable three-level set creating a glitzy bathhouse with 60 doors, ran for a year. In 1975, Moreno received an Antoinette Perry (Tony) Award for Best Supporting Actress in *The Ritz*. Moreno was honored to win, but in her acceptance speech she made it clear that she was very unhappy that her character, who was the centerpiece and inspiration for the play, was considered a supporting, not a leading, role.

Moreno and her husband attend the 1975 Tony Awards ceremony. For her performance in The Ritz, *a zany farce set in a gay bathhouse, Moreno won the theater's most prestigious award, the Tony, for Best Supporting Actress, and the play had a very successful run of 400 performances.*

The success of *The Ritz*, which was performed 400 times, was greatly helped by Moreno's award. The play drew good-sized houses early on, but after she won the Tony the theater was packed and the show's long run assured. One evening, Marlon Brando showed up for a performance, bringing his son Miko and the American Indian Movement leader Dennis Banks. Moreno was concerned about Banks's response to such a bizarre comedy, but he loved it.

Soon, Hollywood became aware of the appeal of Moreno's character. In 1976, a television show based on Googie Gomez, to be called "The Rita Moreno Show," was created as a spin-off of a moderately successful series called "On the Rocks." The pilot was turned down, however, and the show never made the fall schedule. The same fate awaited another pilot framed around Googie in 1977. Comedy writers Mark Rothman and Lowell Ganz, who eventually produced such hits as "Happy Days" and "Laverne and Shirley," created a comedy pilot called "Welcome To Fleckman's" starring Moreno. But it, too, was not picked up by the networks.

A film version of *The Ritz*, however, directed by Richard Lester, was released by Warner in October, 1976. At a party celebrating the premiere of her new movie, Moreno entertained the press as though she were Googie Gomez, wiggling, kissing, and cursing, acting, as one reporter observed dryly, like a Latin spitfire, the stereotype she so often decried. The same reporter noted that the next day at her interview, Moreno was subdued and thoughtful, watching her language and careful not to criticize her director, Richard Lester. Some film critics did not like Lester's handling of Moreno's character and his overall direction of the film, and the film version of *The Ritz* was not nearly as popular as the Broadway show. Nonetheless, the film was important for Moreno because it helped bring her back to Hollywood.

In 1976, the New York chapter of the National Academy of Television Arts and Sciences invited Moreno to address their annual meeting. She accepted the invitation and used the occasion to speak out against excessive violence in television programming. The following year, Moreno performed briefly in a Broadway revival of *She Loves Me* and returned to the Long Wharf in New Haven to play Serafina again in *The Rose Tattoo*. Once again working in television, Moreno played the chief of services at a New York hospital in another unsuccessful pilot. Also in 1977, Moreno hosted a PBS special, "Bilingualism: Asset or Problem in America," about the serious need for bilingual education in America.

Jim Henson, creator of "The Muppets," gave Moreno a call in 1977 and asked her to be a guest star on his very successful children's show. Moreno accepted the offer and flew to London where the episode was filmed. Just as she did on "The Electric Company," Moreno worked with the director to evolve her scenes

Moreno with Jim Henson's Muppets in 1977. That year her performance on "The Muppets" won her the television industry's most coveted award, the Emmy, for Best Performing Artist in a Variety Show.

Moreno won a second Emmy in 1978 for her performance in an episode of "The Rockford Files." The Guinness Book of World Records *lists Moreno as the only performer to win all four top entertainment awards—the Oscar, the Tony, the Grammy, and the Emmy.*

by sharing her ideas about her characters. In one skit, she played a French apache dancer. Usually, in French apache dancing, the man throws the woman around. Moreno's idea was that the roles be reversed, and this was how it was filmed.

The skit was set in a little waterfront dive, where Moreno danced with a life-sized male apache Muppet. When he started flirting with a pig, Moreno grew jealous and, as part of the dance, bashed him all around the café. In another skit, Moreno's character got into a hair-pulling match with Miss Piggy. Moreno's delight and skill in slapstick and broad comedy made the episode sparkle. That year, she won an Emmy, the television industry's equivalent of an Oscar, for Best Performing Artist in a Variety Show.

In 1978, Moreno was cast as an endearing and vulnerable prostitute on the television series "The Rockford Files," starring James Garner. Her performance won an Emmy for Best Guest Actress in a Drama. Audiences were so charmed by her character that Moreno was brought back to play her in two more episodes, one of which earned Moreno an Emmy nomination in the same category. Also that year, Moreno played a Jewish mother in a film called *The Boss's Son* (American Cinema Ltd.).

Rita, Lenny, and Nandy started discussing the possibility of moving back to Los Angeles. Lenny's heart condition was very serious and had caused him to be hospitalized. They reasoned that the mild weather in Los Angeles would be much easier for him than New York's freezing winters and hot, steamy summers. It also looked as if Moreno could continue to do film and television work if they moved. They decided to keep their apartment in New York but to make Los Angeles their new home. In 1979, Rita, Lenny, and 12-year-old Fernanda moved into a house in Los Angeles.

That year the *Guinness Book of World Records* took note of Moreno's achievements and recognized her as the first and, so far, only performer to win all four top entertainment awards—the Oscar, the Grammy, the Tony, and the Emmy. Without a doubt, Rita Moreno had dispelled the so-called curse of the Oscar.

Moreno, as Olive Madison, confronts her overly neat counterpart, Florence Unger, played by Sally Struthers, in The Odd Couple. *In 1985, Neil Simon rewrote the play, originally written for two male characters, so that two women could play the lead roles.*

CHAPTER EIGHT

"I Am an Actress"

In 1978, shortly before she left New York, Moreno decided to put together a one-woman show. The idea of working on a project that was essentially her own had always appealed to her. In fact, she had once created her own act as a teenager. This time, of course, the project would be a much more elaborate enterprise. She hired a choreographer, a music arranger, and a costumer; picked out songs she wanted to sing; and put together a colorful, energetic song and dance show. She debuted her work first in Chicago and then at the Grand Finale II, a club in New York City. Later that year she performed in Hollywood at Scandals Showroom, where she included three male dancers who served as her chorus and foils for her comedy routines. Her show was so well received that soon she was invited to open for Bill Cosby at Harrah's Casino in Lake Tahoe, California.

Moreno continues to evolve her show, which she calls "a god-send . . . which revalidates what my work is all about." Although she does not include rock music in her show, Moreno has an extensive and diverse repertoire. She has performed on luxury cruise ships such as the *Queen Elizabeth II*, at conventions, and at showrooms in such places as Las Vegas, Toronto, and Atlantic City. When she travels, Moreno keeps things simple by taking along only a conductor, a rhythm section, and a sound engineer. Her husband does the booking, runs the lights, and keeps things organized. As she did when she was a teenage Spanish dancer, Moreno still takes along cases of costumes plus her own clothes and accessories.

In 1980, shortly after settling in Los Angeles, Moreno was cast as an Italian-American mistress in *Happy Birthday, Gemini* (United Artists), a film adaptation of the Broadway comedy *Gemini*. The next year, Alan Alda cast Moreno as the wife of the dentist Jack Weston in his film *The Four Seasons* (Universal), about three married couples who take vacations together. Although many critics liked Alda's film and some gave special mention to Moreno's performance, it was not a box office success.

*The 1980s got off to a great start for Moreno, who appeared in two films—*Happy Birthday, Gemini, *in 1980, and* The Four Seasons, *in 1981—before accepting a part in the Broadway comedy* Wally's Café.

Moreno, James Coco, and Sally Struthers in a scene from Wally's Café. *Despite solid work by the cast, the seriously flawed play was lambasted by the critics and ultimately survived only 12 performances.*

With no new films in the offing in 1981, Moreno decided to accept a part in a new Broadway comedy, *Wally's Café*. Despite preview performances that left audiences unenthusiastic and prospects for the play's future dismal, opening night on Broadway was as rich and ritualized as always. Crowds gathered at the Brooks Atkinson Theatre, limousines arrived, and the actors were swamped with flowers and cards. Moreno, calling herself "La Contessa," settled down to put on her makeup. As she worked, she began her vocal exercises. Belting out songs as Googie Gomez in *The Ritz* had left her with problems with her voice, so warming up was important. Moreno and James Coco shouted comments back and forth through the walls of their dressing rooms. They tried to sound enthusiastic and ready to give their best, although they knew the play had serious problems.

This was the first Broadway performance for Sally Struthers, an actress who had become famous as Gloria in the innovative television situation comedy "All in the Family." Fans, reporters, and photographers lavished Struthers with attention, and she loved it. Moreno and James Coco were less taken by all the commotion; they had been through this many times before. A makeup man came in to apply final touches to Moreno's face as, over the intercom, the stage manager announced curtly that the call was in half an hour. The makeup man waved good-bye saying, "Break legs, dahlings!"

When the play was over, the cast came out to take its bows. Everyone knew by the audience's shifting, coughing, and mild applause during the show that it was a flop. Suddenly, Moreno approached the edge of the stage and pulled open her jacket, sticking out her chest in defiance, instead of raising her middle finger as Brando would have done. Her reason was not that she was hot but, as she told a reporter for *Mademoiselle* who covered the opening, to show the critics she did not care.

Afterward, streams of people crowded backstage offering praise and congratulations. Moreno and James Coco knew that this would happen even if the play were poorly received. As usual, the cast, joined by admirers, entered nearby Sardi's restaurant for the expected opening night celebration. As is their custom, the waiters and patrons applauded the entering actors and many jumped to their feet shouting, "Bravo!" Most, of course, had not even seen the play, which ended up running for only 12 performances.

During rehearsals for *Wally's Café*, Jane Fonda called to ask Moreno to do a screen test for Fonda's new television series based on the popular film *9 to 5*. At first, she was annoyed that after so many years on the screen she would be asked to audition. But she realized that the producers would want to check the chemistry among the three principal players, so she consented. Moreno flew to Hollywood exhausted from a strenuous rehearsal schedule, taped her audition, which required her to repeat the same scene 10 times, and caught a plane back to New York. On the way out, Fonda hugged Moreno and told her she had "funny in her bones!"

Moreno looked forward to taping the episodes of "9 to 5" and to working steadily on a successful series. She believed she could stay home with her family when she worked on the series and do theater in the summers. Besides, Moreno liked the premise of the show, especially the way it allowed her to break down stereotypes about middle-aged women. Moreno played the supervising secretary Violet, a widow with two children, which was the part Lily Tomlin played in the film. Moreno told *TV Guide* writer Jack Hicks that she saw her character as a "foxy den mother with brains," who could "show the women out there that you don't shrivel up like a raisin when you hit 40."

"9 to 5" was modestly successful in its initial run during the 1982–83 season. Then the producers changed most of the production staff and the show's time slot. At first the ratings jumped, but then they declined. Eventually, the show was canceled.

Moreno returned her attention to promoting her nightclub act, which she performed as a benefit for various symphony or-

Valerie Curtin, Rachel Dennison, and Rita Moreno starred in the television series "9 to 5," which was aired during 1982 and 1983. Moreno enjoyed the series because it depicted women, particularly women approaching middle age, as bright and capable players in the business world.

chestras, including the San Diego Symphony. When Moreno was the featured performer at a celebration in Hollywood honoring director Robert Wise, who had directed her in *West Side Story*, the crowd jumped to its feet, applauding and calling for more.

In 1984, Moreno and her daughter, Fernanda, performed together at the Sands Hotel in Atlantic City. Fernanda had studied dance since she was a young girl, and she was about to begin her freshman year at Tufts University, in Massachusetts, where she intended to major in theater arts. Moreno and Fernanda performed together again in *The Taming of the Shrew* at the Virginia Beach Shakespeare Festival, and still again at the Williamsburg Shakespeare Theatre in Washington, D.C. In 1990, they performed as mother and daughter in *Steel Magnolias* at the Cherry County Theatre in Traverse City, Michigan.

Fernanda graduated from Tufts with a dual degree in English and theater arts and went on to receive a master of fine arts degree

Moreno and her daughter, backstage at the Virginia Beach Shakespeare Festival. In 1987, Fernanda, who is also pursuing an acting career, appeared with her mother in the festival's production of The Taming of the Shrew.

in theater arts from the University of Southern California. Currently she lives in Los Angeles, where she works as an actress and
maintains her interest in writing. Although Moreno and Lenny
never urged Fernanda into the performing arts, Moreno feels she
has the natural sensitivity of an artist. When Fernanda wanted to
study acting in college, her parents supported her interest and now
support her career in any way they can.

In her next Broadway role—in *The Odd Couple*, which opened at
the Longacre in June 1985—Moreno played Olive Madison, the
sloppy half of the couple, opposite Sally Struthers, who played the
overly neat Florence Unger. Neil Simon rewrote the play so that two
women could play the lead roles. This version of the play was
moderately successful, with critics split over the revision that cast
two women in the leads instead of men. Most agreed, however, that
Moreno played her role with finesse.

In November 1988, Moreno starred in a PBS hour-long television film, "The Closed Set," part of a series called "Tales from the
Hollywood Hills." Moreno played Julie Forbes, a movie star who
hires an art film director to make a film that would save her sagging
career. Moreno's performance was based on her personal obser-
vations of movie queens like Joan Crawford and Lana Turner, both
of whom could be drippingly sweet one minute and bitingly
cruel the next. In interviews about the show, Moreno praised PBS
for employing women—who are extremely underemployed in the
film and television industry—as producer, director, and writer for
this film.

Since 1988, Moreno has been helping to raise production
money for *Hearts on Fire*, the first film to be written, directed,
and produced by Hispanic women. The film, which will feature
Moreno, Ed Asner, and Edward James Olmos, tells the story of the
filming of the 1954 movie *Salt of the Earth*. This film, about a New
Mexico miners' strike led by Hispanic women, was made, despite
severe political pressure, by film industry people blacklisted by the
House Un-American Activities Committee in the 1950s. The House
of Representatives set up this committee as a response to Senator

Joseph McCarthy's campaign against what he perceived as the subversion of American industries and institutions by Communist sympathizers.

Women's magazines often interview Moreno about her health and beauty secrets. In 1991, she put out an exercise video, "Now You Can," which *Lear's* magazine put at the top of their list of the 12 exercise videos by and for women over the age of 35. Moreno says her "secrets" are not worrying about her age (which she will gladly tell), daily exercise, plenty of rest, and a healthy diet, in that order. She is convinced, too, that a happy attitude is central to looking and feeling good. Moreno commented in *USA Weekend* magazine that "when you're young, bad things seem like the end of the world. Later, you realize you don't die from adversity."

Discussing her one-woman show, Moreno told an interviewer for the *Chicago Tribune*, "There used to be this notion that once you're over 35 you're over the hill. I can't tell you how many young men come backstage with the most amazed look on their faces muttering 'Hey, you're foxy!' Why shouldn't I be?" Having reached 60, Moreno made it a point to talk about her age as part of her show. In a performance at Big Bear Lake, California, she charmed her audience with her clear, emotionally affecting voice, slim figure, and her ability to create an intimate atmosphere in a large theater. Toward the end of the performance, Moreno reminded everyone who was not yet 60 that they would be someday. Then she pointed to her buttocks, her belly, and her arms, all firmly toned, and observed that being 60 does not mean you have to look baggy or flabby. Regular exercise is the key, Moreno advised.

Moreno credits the experience of raising her daughter for challenging her attitudes about what it means to be a woman. Confronting her own feelings of never being good enough, her reliance on men, and her need to always be the "good little girl," she has wanted Fernanda to grow up with a clear and independent sense of herself. Moreno stays in touch with her mother, who lives with her fifth husband in a Southern California retirement community.

Moreno and her mother share a moment on the set of "9 to 5" in 1982. In the early 1990s, Rosa María was living with her fifth husband in a Southern California retirement community, and Rita was regularly in touch with her.

In 1989, Moreno took a leading role in another television series, playing Burt Reynolds's former wife, Kimberly Baskin, in the detective series "B. L. Stryker." Some critics felt Moreno was miscast. Others, who praised her work in an otherwise slow-moving show, found it hard to believe that she could play a character called Kimberly. To Moreno this typifies her struggle with what she calls "the attitude." Recalling the many types of characters she has played on stage, Moreno insists that on TV or in film "I should be able to play any part I can do well. I am an actress."

Moreno still faces racial and sexist stereotyping. In 1989 her agent sent her to read for a part as an eccentric, non-Hispanic, aging actress in a film to star Kevin Costner. But when she arrived to do her reading, the director told her that he wanted her to play a Mexican whorehouse madam, a role with a few lines in Spanish and even fewer in English. Momentarily devastated, Moreno took a breath to hold back her tears, told him off, and left. Luis Avalos observed, "Sometimes the only thing you can do is turn down work. And if you turn down work, aside from not making money, you're simply not working at what you love most. Also, the more you work, the more you work. People need to see you. The decision to not work is not one that is taken lightly. Yet sometimes it has to be done."

Moreno's outspoken concern for Hispanic causes and her numerous public service announcements in Spanish, her developing awareness of her role as a woman, and her support of the arts, along with the breadth of her artistic accomplishments, have created a special place for her in the history of the performing arts. Beginning in 1988, when she and the acclaimed Cuban actor Cesar Romero were given the Bilingual Foundation of the Arts Award, Moreno has been honored by numerous organizations. Again in 1988, she was inducted into the National Hispanic Hall of Fame. She was even elected to succeed Chevy Chase as the honorary mayor of Pacific Palisades, where she has lived for several years. In 1990, when she turned 59, Moreno was honored by the Hispanic Congressional Caucus and received a Distinguished Artist Award from Club 100 of the Los Angeles Music Center. That year she was also honored by the Los Angeles Arts Council.

From a child who dreamed of being Lana Turner, Moreno has evolved into a unique and accomplished performing artist who takes great pride in her Hispanic heritage as well as in being a woman. From New York to Hollywood and back, in the face of racist and sexist stereotyping, Moreno's career has defied the odds. "The most poignant struggle on earth," Moreno observes, "is the struggle to survive no matter what happens." Moreno's Puerto Rican heritage, especially her jibaro roots, is infused with the spirit of the island's Borinquén Indian women, whose resilience was legendary. Moreno's life is a testament to that spirit.

In the 1980s and 1990s, Rita Moreno not only continued to enjoy success in theater, film, and television, but she also became more committed than ever to raising public awareness of Hispanic culture, improving education for America's children, and supporting the arts.

Selected Filmography

1950   *So Young So Bad*
        United Artists

        The Toast of New Orleans
        MGM

        Pagan Love Song
        MGM

1952   *The Fabulous Señorita*
        Republic

        The Ring
        King Brothers

        Cattle Town
        Warner

        Singin' in the Rain
        MGM

1953   *El Alamein*
        Columbia

        Fort Vengeance
        Allied Artists

        Latin Lovers
        MGM

        Jivaro
        Paramount

1954   *The Yellow Tomahawk*
United Artists

Garden of Evil
20th Century Fox

1955   *Untamed*
20th Century Fox

Seven Cities of Gold
20th Century Fox

The Lieutenant Wore Skirts
20th Century Fox

1956   *The King and I*
20th Century Fox

The Vagabond King
Paramount

1957   *The Deerslayer*
20th Century Fox

1960   *This Rebel Breed*
Warner

1961   *Summer and Smoke*
Paramount

West Side Story
United Artists

1963   *Cry of Battle*
Allied Artists

1969   *The Night of the Following Day*
        Universal

        Marlowe
        MGM/Katzka-Berne-Cherokee/Beckerman

        Popi
        United Artists/Leonard Films

1971   *Carnal Knowledge*
        Avco-Embassy/Icarus

1976   *The Ritz*
        Warner/Courtyard

1978   *The Boss' s Son*
        American Cinema Ltd.

1980   *Happy Birthday, Gemini*
        United Artists

1981   *The Four Seasons*
        Universal

Chronology

December 11, 1931	Born Rosa Dolores Alverio, in Humacao, Puerto Rico
1936	Moves to New York with her mother, Rosa María, leaving her father and brother behind
1944	Moves with her mother and second stepfather, Edward Moreno, to Valley Stream, Long Island; debuts as Angelina in *Skydrift*, her first Broadway play
1948	Meets Louis B. Mayer and is signed to a contract with MGM
1949	Plays a delinquent in her first film, *So Young So Bad*
1950	Moves to Los Angeles with her family; parents get divorced. Changes her name to Rita Moreno; debuts as Tina in *The Toast of New Orleans* with Mario Lanza; MGM contract not renewed
1952–54	Makes several Westerns; begins her relationships with Marlon Brando and George A. Hormel

1954	Appears on the cover of *Life* magazine; signed by 20th Century Fox
1955–56	Makes a series of films for Fox, including *The King and I*
1957–60	Begins a career in regional theater and summer stock
1960	Films *Summer and Smoke* and *West Side Story*
1961	Attempts suicide
1962	Wins the Oscar for Best Supporting Actress in *West Side Story*; donates money toward an acting scholarship at the University of Puerto Rico
1963	Moves to London, England
1964	Moves to New York to take a starring role in *The Sign in Sidney Brustein's Window*
June 18, 1965	Marries Leonard Gordon
1967	Gives birth to a daughter, Fernanda Luisa
April 4, 1968	Receives Joseph Jefferson Award for her portrayal of Serafina in *The Rose Tattoo*
1969–71	Plays supporting role in *The Night of the Following Day*, her first film in several years; also cast in *Marlowe*, *Popi*, and *Carnal Knowledge*
1970	Stars in *The Last of the Red Hot Lovers* on Broadway

1971	Joins the cast of "The Electric Company"
1972	Wins a Grammy, along with the rest of the cast, for a sound track recording of "The Electric Company"
1975	*The Ritz*, based on Moreno's Googie Gomez character, is a hit on Broadway and earns her a Tony
1976	Warner releases a film version of *The Ritz*
1977	Moreno wins an Emmy for her work as a guest artist on an episode of "The Muppets"
1978	Wins another Emmy for her portrayal of a vulnerable prostitute on "The Rockford Files"; opens her one-woman nightclub show
1979	Moreno and her family move to Los Angeles; *Guinness Book of World Records* notes her as the only performer to win all four top entertainment awards
1980	Moreno appears in the films *Happy Birthday, Gemini* and *The Four Seasons*
1981	Is cast in a Broadway comedy, "Wally's Café"
1982	Appears in the television series "9 to 5"
1984	Performs for the first time with her daughter, Fernanda
1985	Appears in the Broadway play *The Odd Couple*

| 1989 | Plays a leading role in the television series "B. L. Stryker" |
| 1988–92 | Makes numerous television appearances and continues to perform her one-woman show; receives several awards honoring her contribution to the arts and to the Hispanic community; puts out an exercise video |

Further Reading

Acker, Ally. *Reel Women: Pioneers of the Cinema, 1986 to the Present.* New York: Continuum, 1990.

Bonavoglia, Angela. *The Choices We Made: 25 Women and Men Speak Out About Choice.* New York: Random House, 1991.

Hadley-Garcia, George. *Hispanic Hollywood: The Latins in Motion Pictures.* New York: Carol Publishing Group, 1990.

Higham, Charles. *Brando: The Unauthorized Biography.* New York: New American Library, 1987.

Moore, Joan, and Harry Pacheon. *Hispanics in the United States.* Englewood Cliffs, NJ: Prentice Hall, 1985.

Steiner, Stan. *The Islands: The World of the Puerto Ricans.* New York: HarperCollins, 1974.

Thomas, Piri. *Down These Mean Streets.* New York: Knopf, 1967.

Woll, Allen L. *The Latin Image in American Film.* Rev. ed. Los Angeles: UCLA Latin American Center Publications, 1980.

Index

SUSAN SUNTREE is a graduate of the University of Arizona and received an M.A. in English from the University of Kent, in Canterbury, England. Her publications include a book of poetry, *Eye of the Womb*. In 1990 she helped translate *Tulips*, a collection of poems by the Spanish poet Ana Rossetti. She lives in Santa Monica, California, and teaches English at East Los Angeles College.

RODOLFO CARDONA is professor of Spanish and comparative literature at Boston University. A renowned scholar, he has written many works of criticism, including *Ramón, a Study of Gómez de la Serna and His Works* and *Visión del esperpento: Teoría y práctica del esperpento en Valle-Inclán*. Born in San José, Costa Rica, he earned his B.A. and M.A. from Louisiana State University and received a Ph.D. from the University of Washington. He has taught at Case Western Reserve University, the University of Pittsburgh, the University of Texas at Austin, the University of New Mexico, and Harvard University.

JAMES COCKCROFT is currently a visiting professor of Latin American and Caribbean studies at the State University of New York at Albany. A three-time Fulbright scholar, he earned a Ph.D. from Stanford University and has taught at the University of Massachusetts, the University of Vermont, and the University of Connecticut. He is the author or coauthor of numerous books on Latin American subjects, including *Neighbors in Turmoil: Latin America, The Hispanic Experience in the United States: Contemporary Issues and Perspectives*, and *Outlaws in the Promised Land: Mexican Immigrant Workers and America's Future*.